George P. Mitchell and the Idea of Sustainability

George P. Mitchell

and the Idea of Sustainability

Jurgen Schmandt

TEXAS A&M UNIVERSITY PRESS • COLLEGE STATION

Manufactured in the United States of America
All rights reserved
First edition

This paper meets the requirements of ANSI/NISO
Z39.48-1992 (Permanence of Paper).
Binding materials have been chosen for durability.
∞
Library of Congress Cataloging-in-Publication Data
Schmandt, Jurgen.
George P. Mitchell and the idea of sustainability /
Jurgen Schmandt.—1st ed.
      p. cm.
  Includes bibliographical references and index.
  ISBN-13: 978-1-60344-217-6 (hc stamped with
jacket : alk. paper)
  ISBN-10: 1-60344-217-0 (hc stamped with jacket :
alk. paper) 1. Mitchell, George P. (George Phydias),
1919– 2. Sustainable development—History.
3. Businesspeople—Texas. 4. Philanthropists—
Texas. I. Title.
  HC110.E5S395 2010
  338.9'27092—dc22

                                    2010016587

*All photos are courtesy of the Houston Advanced
Research Center and the George P. Mitchell family.*

This story is for my grandchildren who will help create a more sustainable world: Nicolaus, Danielle, Mike, Cyra, Henry, Dennis, and Lily

CONTENTS

PREFACE

This book tells two stories. The first one is devoted to sustainability—what it is and how the idea grew over time. To develop the story I cite key authors who contributed to the sustainability debate during the last half century: Rachel Carson, Garret Hardin, Paul Ehrlich, Ian McHarg, Buckminster Fuller, Ken Boulding, Dennis and Donella Meadows, E. F. Schumacher, Herman Daly, Eleanor Ostrom, Jim MacNeill, Gus Speth, Robert Kates, William Clark, and Lester Brown. I will also look back in time and retrace the early history of sustainability, which, as best as I can see, started some two hundred years ago. This provides the context for my main story, which tells how several of the above-mentioned scholars, through direct contact or through their written work, inspired George P. Mitchell to build a unique program in support of sustainability. Mitchell is a business leader who built a Fortune 500 company. His initiatives in support of sustainability span four decades. They stand out as a model for linking entrepreneurial success to the sustainability movement.

My ideal readers are Mitchell's children and grandchildren and young men and women around the world. I want them to better understand sustainability and why George Mitchell—as family man and citizen—invested such a large amount of time and money into sustainability projects. Hopefully, this knowledge will inspire the younger generation to continue Mitchell's journey toward sustainability. It is they who must move us from sustainability research and planning, where we have made progress, to building sustainable societies, where we are lagging behind.

The number of studies, reports and conferences on sustainable development is by now substantial. With few exceptions I will deal only with those in which my two stories—the intellectual history of sustainable development and the work of George Mitchell—meet. As I will show, this happened repeatedly. By and large I follow a chronological order and switch between chapters devoted to sustainability and chapters focused on the actions of George Mitchell. Thus the linkages between my two stories will emerge clearly.

The plan of the book is as follows. In the introduction I define sustainability. Chapter 1 introduces George P. Mitchell as a captain of industry, builder of a green city, and thinker who deeply cares about the future of mankind. In chapter 2 I discuss how the idea of sustainability evolved. Chapter 3 explains why sustainable development is needed more today than in earlier times. Chapter 4 tells how the Club of Rome, in the late 1960s, started a worldwide campaign to draw attention to unsustainable aspects of the modern world, which in their opinion resulted from uncontrolled population growth and too much of a good thing—economic growth. Chapter 5 recounts how Mitchell joined forces with the Club of Rome, and created the Woodlands Conference series and the Mitchell Prize for Sustainable Development. Chapter 6 describes early efforts by the U.S. federal government and the nongovernmental World Resources Institute to develop policy in support of sustainability. Chapter 7 is an account of the sustainability program that Mitchell created at the Houston Advanced Research Center (HARC). Chapter 8 is devoted to Mitchell's work with the National Academy of Sciences, which defined the role of science in building sustainable societies. Chapter 9 reviews recent reforms of Mitchell's sustainability program at HARC. Chapter 10 asks whether and how Mitchell reconciled his careers in energy and real estate development with his commitment to sustainability. Chapter 11 summarizes Mitchell's impact on the sustainability movement and his continuing legacy.

The reader should know that I have worked with George Mitchell for over twenty years, first as director in charge of sustainability studies and conferences at the Houston Advanced Research Center, and now as a consultant working with the Cynthia and George Mitchell Foundation. To prepare this book I conducted seven in-depth interviews with Mr. Mitchell in the spring of 2006 and the fall of 2007. In 2007 I dug into the Mitchell company archives and, together with Grant Mitchell, interviewed individuals with whom Mitchell had worked when designing his sustainability projects. These include Shere Abbott, Bruce Alberts, Cabell Brand, Ralph Cicerone, E. William Colglazier, Pamela Matson, Dennis Meadows, Frank Press, Peter Raven, and George Symmes. In 2008 we conducted a survey of Mitchell Prize laureates. Transcripts and videotapes of the interviews are on file with the Mitchell Family Foundation.

I benefited from the comments on my numerous drafts by George P. Mitchell, members of his family, and anonymous reviewers at Texas A&M University Press. My editor, Shannon Davies, helped greatly with streamlining the text. Susan Weeks conducted the survey of Mitchell Prize winners and helped with other tasks. Robert Harriss provided insightful comments on the direction HARC is taking under his leadership. I am much obliged to them. I also thank Meredith Dreiss (née Mitchell), Grant Mitchell, and Todd Mitchell for their support, comments, and patience. They took great care in reviewing my drafts. Todd, in addition, helped me to understand "the Mitchell Paradox."

The views expressed in this book are entirely mine.

INTRODUCTION

The Idea of Sustainability

This book is about making modern societies more sustainable than they are today and about one man's efforts—George P. Mitchell—to move us toward this goal. There are many definitions of sustainability. Most agree on three points: People should not consume renewable resources beyond nature's capacity to replenish stocks; the present generation should limit consumption of finite resources so that their children can meet their own needs in the future; and development should link environmental protection to improving quality of life and reducing human poverty. Over time, priorities of what needs to be constrained and what needs to be sustained have shifted. In the sixties the focus was on reducing pollution of the air, water, and land. The goal was to clean up the environment. In the seventies population growth and the looming scarcity of natural resources took center stage. The goal was to ensure long-term availability of natural resources. The eighties focused on acid rain, ozone depletion, and toxic substances in the environment. The goal was to reduce threats to the environment and to human health. The nineties began to zero in on climate change, an issue that remains at the heart of the sustainability debate today. The challenge is to balance demographic and economic growth with the protection of natural systems that sustain life. It is this interface between nature and society that best describes the nature of sustainability. I offer the following definition: *Sustainable societies seek and maintain a careful balance between economic and ecological well-being. Economic well-being provides for the necessities of human life (jobs, food, shelter, sanitation, and energy). Ecological well-being sustains the natural systems on which all life depends.*

People have long faced scarcity or destruction of the natural resources they depend on, such as food, wood, and water. In the past these threats occurred at local or regional scales. They did not impact the planet as a whole. Today's situation is more challenging. Global warming, the most prominent threat to sustainability the world has encountered so far, is caused by the rapid industrialization of a vastly increased human population; it impacts all regions and continents, though in different ways. This difference in scale and diversity of impacts explains why today's problems are more complex and difficult to resolve. But to get started I will use two simple examples, taken from the Middle Ages, to illustrate how human action can endanger important natural resources.

The first example is based on an often-quoted essay published in 1968, at the very beginning of the debate about sustainability. *The Tragedy of the Commons*, by Garret Hardin, is a great introduction to understanding sustainability.[1] It tells the story of how a shared natural resource, the English village commons, was destroyed by overuse. In medieval English villages, a parcel of land called the commons was set aside for open grazing. All villagers had free access. Medieval society was hierarchically structured: villagers provided for the needs of the upper classes—nobility and clergy—through hard manual labor. Villagers "worked for all," nobles "fought for all," and priests "prayed for all." A large portion of the villagers' time was spent working the lord's land, and much of the villagers' income they earned from working the land for themselves went to fees and taxes. To make ends meet, villagers had to gain some untaxed income from raising a cow or a goat on the village commons. The medieval rural system was built on the equitable exploitation of this shared resource. The villagers were encouraged to fatten their cattle on the commons so that they, as well as the village as a whole, benefited. The commons was a cornerstone of rural life.

At some point, at first barely perceptible, this benefit was endangered. As the number of villagers increased, more cattle grazed on the commons, eventually leading to overgrazing. This had to be stopped to avoid destruction of the commons. The villagers faced a choice: they could continue the practice of free access, but by doing so they would gradually destroy the commons. Or they could heed early signs of trouble and agree among themselves to curb the use of the commons. Individual restraint, exercised by all, would still give grazing rights to all villagers but at a reduced rate. A small personal sacrifice would protect the commons and make it sustainable. Instead, the villagers made no changes. Ignoring early signs of damage eventually led to tragedy, defined by Hardin as "the remorseless working of things." The tragic destruction of the commons resulted from the villagers' insistence that each individual's right of access was sacrosanct even if the larger number of villagers could no longer support this practice.

In Hardin's view the only viable way to save the commons was to adopt mutually agreed upon rules that restricted the use of the commons—a moral and legal decision, not a technical one. To save the commons the villagers would have to adopt rules that responded to an increase in their numbers.

Hardin emphasizes at the outset that sustainability, once lost, can be restored if people make timely decisions to reverse course. Citing continued rapid population growth as the dominant problem threatening the future of humankind, Hardin wrote: "The population problem has no technical solution; it requires a fundamental extension in morality." This is a key insight about the nature of sustainability: Threats to sustainability that are caused by human behavior—not by natural disasters—can be overcome by taking timely action to change the offensive behavior. I call this the first principle of sustainability: *Sustainability is a moral and behavioral concept.* Technical solutions will help but only if they are supported by value changes. Second, Hardin identifies critical steps on the path from good to bad, up to the point in time when people face a critical choice. It is at this moment that sustainability can be restored or lost forever. This is the second principle of sustainability: *Sustainability is a process, not a steady state.* The critical questions, in the middle ages as today, are these: Are people willing to heed early warnings and change their ways? Will they insist on preserving time-honored rights or are they willing to cut back in the interest of the common good? Are early warning signs, even when information about damage is still incomplete, viewed as an excuse for doing nothing or as the signal for taking action before it is too late? In the case of the English commons the outcome is well known. What had been communal property became enclosed (privatized), and the lifestyle of the peasantry, and society as a whole, was changed forever.

When Hardin wrote *The Tragedy of the Commons*, the term sustainable development was not yet in use. But his essay perfectly describes the critical steps in the transition from a sustainable to an unsustainable state: At the outset things work fine, then warning flags go up, change is called for, but the people ignore dire predictions and continue to do business as usual. In the end the resource is destroyed and people's lives change for the worse. There are agonizing questions to be faced as the story unfolds: When is the right time to change course? Is the evidence strong enough to do so? How do we know that the outcome will be as devastating as the experts predict? Am I willing to give up part of my right as a condition for maintaining the common resource? And if I agree to do so, will my neighbor do the same, or will he cheat?

Here is a second example. Jared Diamond, in *Collapse*, his book of richly documented case studies of past ecological disasters, compares the fate of two groups of people living in the same environment—the Inuit and the Vikings.[2] For centuries they lived side by side in Greenland but developed entirely different lifestyles. The Inuit adapted to the harsh natural environment by relying on the resources offered by the sea. They live there to this day. The Vikings imported Scandinavian-style agriculture and husbandry. They despised the Inuit as inferior. Eventually, the climate turned colder, vegetation suffered, the sheep destroyed the grazing grounds, and the Vikings, unwilling to live like the Inuit, starved to death. Collapse was not inevitable. They simply refused to make the decisions that would have allowed them to survive.

In Hardin's story the right solution is reducing one's share. In Diamond's account more is at stake: changing an entire traditional lifestyle. Here is the all-important conclusion: Sustainability, once lost, could have been restored by reforms in the case of the medieval villagers. The Vikings, however, needed to make fundamental changes in vision, law, behavior, and technology. Revolutions of this kind happen rarely; they require leadership, an enlightened citizenry, and real sacrifice on everyone's part.

The two examples of past tragedies were the result of local problems. Today, problems are both global and local in scale. The interaction between global natural and local social systems defines today's challenge. The world came to this point by success. Over the course of the last three centuries the people of the industrialized world invented ever more powerful technologies to develop national and eventually global economies. They did so at a faster pace than ever before. Many countries benefited, getting wealthier and healthier. Developing countries increased in numbers but remained poor. Overall, the human condition progressed more than anyone could have imagined at the beginning of the industrial age. In the process people acquired the power to alter the global commons—the atmosphere, the ozone layer, the oceans, rain forests, wildlife, and water. This was not intended but happened as the unforeseen result of population growth, technological change, and higher levels of consumption. Many experts now believe that protection and restoration of the global commons is the essence of sustainability. For others the highest priority is the reduction of poverty. Still others focus on the need to conserve natural resources in order to avoid critical shortages of food, fuels, and minerals. In the grand vision all three goals—environmental, social, and economic—come together.

As human population grew in numbers critical questions began to be asked: Can progress go too far? When is such a point reached? Ever since 1962, when Rachel Carson published *Silent Spring*, scholars have presented evidence that humankind has reached a point where continued success—defined as more quantitative economic growth and consumption—produces undesirable side effects. Initially, scholars like Carson pointed to damage to wildlife, in the 1970s scarcity of natural resources, such as food and minerals, moved to center stage. From the 1980s forward, scientists have warned that rapid development will endanger the proper functioning of natural systems on which life depends, particularly the atmosphere, ozone layer, and oceans.

What do these warnings mean for the future of humankind? Obviously, people must always strive for the necessities of life—jobs, shelter, food, and security. As the number of people grows, the demand for these necessities will also grow. But providing for a larger population may only be possible if citizens and governments also take action to address the new problems that have arisen as byproducts of progress: overuse of natural resources, loss of biodiversity, climate change, depletion of the ozone layer, deforestation, and salinization and desertification of land. These problems result from the impact of human actions on nature. There may not be enough jobs, shelter, food, and security for future generations unless these growth problems are brought under control. *This is the essence of today's quest for sustainability: to make economic growth and social progress compatible with the laws governing the natural environment.* Our situation today, I believe, is as challenging as for the Vikings in the past.

Jeffrey Sachs, director of the Earth Institute at Columbia University and of the United Nations Millennium Project, writes: "Our era, I believe, will be dominated by the geopolitics of sustainability."[3] In his view governments, international organizations, nonprofits, and individuals must take action to maintain and restore the conditions that support life for humans as well as for other species living on this planet. During the last half century scientists have learned a great deal about the new problems resulting from growth and what needs to be done to restore sustainability. Yet the world has made limited progress in translating scientific findings into action. Sachs argues, and I believe he is right, that sustainability must now rise to the top of the political agenda. If this were to happen sustainability would join the policy priorities of the past two centuries—industrial innovation, economic growth, and social security. The stories of the village commons and of Greenland contain a sobering warning: The sustainability of human societies—and ultimately the survival of the human species—will depend on people making radical changes and sacrifices.

At Bettison's fishing pier in Galveston, Texas, fifteen-year-old George Mitchell, at 110 pounds, is outweighed by the 120-pound tarpon he caught.

George Mitchell in his Aggie cadet uniform, at the time of his graduation from Texas A&M University. He has continued to be a strong supporter of his alma mater.

The Mitchells with their children, outside their home in Houston in the 1960s.

Young George and Cynthia Mitchell pose on the beach in Galveston.

Donella Meadows, lead author of the *Limits to Growth* report, gives her paper "The Trade-Off between Agricultural Growth and Equity in the Third World" at the 1975 Woodlands Conference.

Hazel Henderson, prominent futurist from Princeton University, speaks at the 1975 Woodlands Conference, giving a paper entitled "Beyond Economics: Energetics and the Conceptual Limits of Quantitative Methodology."

World Watch Institute president Lester Brown, member of the food limits panel at the 1975 Woodlands Conference, gives a paper called "Gaining Ground."

Alexander King, director of the Organization for Economic Cooperation and Development, and cofounder of the Club of Rome, moderates a plenary session at the 1977 Woodlands Conference.

Dennis Meadows, coauthor of *The Limits to Growth* and member of the Woodlands Conference board of directors, chairs a workshop entitled "Social Structures in a Sustainable State" at the 1977 Woodlands Conference.

Aurelio Peccei, Italian industrialist, scholar, and cofounder of the Club of Rome, chairs a workshop on "Modern Corporations in a Sustainable Society" at the 1977 Woodlands Conference.

At the 1979 Woodlands Conference, George Mitchell (right) and Harlan Cleveland, of the Aspen Institute, sit on either side of Paul Ehrlich, first-place Mitchell Prize winner and population specialist from Stanford University.

Texas Democratic senator Lloyd Bentsen gives an address, "Economic Underpinnings of Sustainable Growth," at the 1979 Woodlands Conference.

Herman Daly, an ecological economist from Louisiana State University, chairs a panel on "Social and Political Aspects of a Sustainable Society."

Orville Freeman and Ruth Karen, coauthors of the paper "The Farmer and the Money Economy," receive the first-place Mitchell Prize award at the 1982 Woodlands Conference.

Hunter Lovins, coauthor of the second-prize paper "Electric Utilities: Key to Capitalizing the Energy Transition," at the 1982 Woodlands Conference.

Jorge Bustamante, director general of the Center for Northern Mexico Border Studies, talks with George Mitchell at the 1985 conference on U.S.–Mexico technology transfer.

George Mitchell introduces the dinner speaker, former President Jimmy Carter, at the 1985 conference, "Technology Transfer: U.S.–Mexico Perspectives."

Mitchell Prize winners and HARC employees at the 1991 Woodlands Conference. From left to right (first row): Antônio Magalhães (third prize), Diana Liverman (second prize), Vijaya Ruby Saha (third prize), Cynthia Mitchell, George Mitchell, Daniel Botkin (first prize), José Goldemberg (second prize). From left to right (back row): Arthur "Skip" Porter, Jurgen Schmandt.

Cynthia and George Mitchell with first-place Mitchell Prize winner at the 1997 Woodlands Conference: Marcelo C. de Andrade, chairman and founder of Pro-Natura, Rio de Janeiro and New York City.

Ray C. Anderson, founder and chairman of Interface, Inc., in Atlanta, Georgia, is presented the first-place Mitchell Prize by Cynthia and George Mitchell at the 2001 Woodlands Conference.

Winners of the 1997 Young Scholars Award with Cynthia and George Mitchell. From left to right: Jayesh Bhatia, Laszlo Pinter, Elizabeth Conover, Alastair Iles, Katrina Smith Korfmacher, Cynthia Mitchell, George Mitchell, Christopher Carr, Pierre Desrochers, Andrew Seidl, Mitch Mathis.

The Mitchells with their children in the 1980s.

The extended Mitchell family at a family gathering.

CHAPTER 1

George P. Mitchell

Early Years

George Phydias Mitchell was born in 1919 in Galveston, Texas. His parents were first-generation immigrants from Greece. His father could neither read nor write. He first worked as a laborer on a railroad gang. One day the foreman told him that his Greek name, Savvas Paraskevopoulos, was too difficult. He named him Mike Mitchell.

George grew up in Galveston with two brothers and a sister. By then his father made a modest living from a clothes-pressing shop and shoeshine parlor. George was a good student, and he loved fishing, hunting, and playing tennis on the public courts. His mother hoped he would become a medical doctor, but his intellectual interests lay elsewhere. The nature of the universe fascinated him, and he dreamed of studying astronomy. In the end, however, he went to Texas A&M University to study petroleum engineering and geology. This career choice promised a more reliable income—certainly a valid consideration for the future father of ten.

Since the discovery of oil in Texas—at Spindletop in 1901 and in East Texas in 1930—the state's economy had been dominated by the oil, gas, and petrochemical industries. In addition to technical knowledge, George's professors gave him practical and ethical advice: Upon completing his studies a good petroleum engineer should strike out in business for himself. One professor made a remark that was far ahead of its time: He should realize that oil and gas were limited resources and make conservation part of his management practice. George excelled in his studies, graduating first in his class. Gaining skills both as an engineer and a geologist would prove most important for his career. He also did well in tennis, and he captained and played on the A&M varsity team. Tennis remained a lifelong passion.

Mitchell Energy and Development Corporation

After military service in the U.S. Army Corps of Engineers—he reached the rank of major—Mitchell acted on his professors' recommendations. In 1946 he began a career as a consulting geologist and petroleum engineer in Houston, the oil capital of Texas. He and his brother Johnny bought into a small exploration firm that enjoyed early successes. The firm discovered a gas field in North Texas that eventually became one of the largest gas fields in North America and the backbone of the company for years to come.[1] Before long, George and Johnny bought out their partners, and the firm prospered and grew, as Mitchell put it, in "geometric dimensions." In 1972 Mitchell Energy and Development Corporation (MND) went public, its stock trading on the American Stock Exchange. George retained over 60 percent ownership in the company. Employment reached four thousand in the early 1980s, and MND became a Fortune 500 company. In 1992, after the company had recovered from the oil bust of the 1980s, trading was transferred to the New York Stock Exchange.

In the 1980s and 1990s Mitchell Energy pioneered the technology of horizontal drilling. Combined with hydraulic fracturing of rock—a technique known since the 1940s—horizontal drilling made it possible to economically extract natural gas from shale rock formations. This breakthrough, in the shale play known as the Barnett Shale, has since been widely adopted by the gas industry and has spawned a new gas boom in North America that has substantially increased the supply of natural gas well into the future. A 2008 report by the Potential Gas Committee, a volunteer nonprofit organization supported by the Colorado School of Mines, estimated that U.S. recoverable supplies will last 118 years at current production levels.[2] A 2009 report, funded by the American Clean Skies Foundation and conducted by Navigant Consulting Inc., supports these findings and attributes the large increase in reserves to "clean-burning fuel trapped in ... shale rock."[3] Natural gas emits about half the carbon dioxide, or CO_2—the principal greenhouse gas—as coal for the same amount of energy produced. For decades to come, therefore, natural gas will play an important role in U.S. efforts to reduce greenhouse emissions and increase energy independence.

The significance of Mitchell Energy's accomplishment is difficult to overstate. The Potential Gas Committee's 2008 report states that "the United

States possesses a total resource base of 1,836 trillion cubic feet. This is the highest resource evaluation in the Committee's 44-year history. Most of the increase from the previous assessment arose from reevaluation of shale-gas plays in the Appalachian basin and in the Mid-Continent, Gulf Coast and Rocky Mountain areas." What is notable is that, as late as the early 1990s, shale gas resources were not considered significant a part of the national resource mix.

Natural gas supplies that are more abundant than previously understood represent an opportunity to reduce greenhouse gas emissions in the United States. Currently, the United States generates twice as much electricity from coal as from natural gas. One analyst suggests that the new abundance of shale gas could allow a doubling of natural gas power generation in the United States, supplanting coal, with a resulting decrease in CO_2 emissions of 330 million tons. This would represent a 5 percent reduction of the United States' net emissions.[4] These emissions reductions can be captured more easily than through policies aimed at stimulating renewable power generation, because the underlying economics are favorable and would require fewer subsidies.

Mitchell, who has been called the "Father of Shale Gas,"[5] proudly recognizes the importance of natural gas for improving U.S. energy policy. "It makes sense to cut down CO_2. We have plenty of gas here and we don't have to send our dollars overseas."[6] It is probably no exaggeration to say that without Mitchell's development of new technology in the pursuit of the natural gas in the Barnett Shale, the potential to reduce CO_2 emissions on a large scale might have taken a decade or two longer to realize with existing technology. Mitchell is intensely proud of the contribution his company made to improving the energy security of the country and, simultaneously, to slowing global warming. Even so, Mitchell's deep interest in sustainable development was focused outside his energy company, as subsequent chapters will show.

Mitchell's success in the energy field was the result of hard work, informed risk taking, team building, and persistent pursuit of new business opportunities. And then there was foresight. Michel Halbouty, himself a highly successful geologist and petroleum engineer, described Mitchell as one of the rare "oil finders." An oil finder is "someone that has the knack, someone that has the deduction, someone that has the inner relationship to the earth, that [is] able to understand what he is looking for."[7] Mitchell put it less dramatically: "You just have to have, first, good technical skills and then understand the geology and the potential … Because I was knowledgeable in both geology and engineering, I was able to see things that the geologists alone couldn't see or the engineers couldn't see."[8] Shaker Khayatt, the banker who prepared the MND public stock offering, offered this: "The first thing that impressed me was Mitchell's vision.… [He] thinks in decades instead of six months.… Here was a man who, with a straight face, told me what the world would be like ten to twenty years into the future. The world according to Mitchell."[9]

In 2002 Mitchell sold his company to Devon Energy for $3.5 billion. In 2009 Forbes included him as number 128 on the list of America's billion-aires, with a net worth of $3.2 billion. The MND story has been told by Joseph Kutchin, long-time vice president of communications for the company.[10]

City in the Woods

With the energy business experiencing periodic ups and downs, Mitchell wanted a second leg for his company and focused on real estate. Initially, he dabbled in real estate development in Galveston, Aspen, and Austin. Then he began to buy land near Houston, first on a small scale but eventually reaching for the sky.

Mitchell's investments in real estate occurred during the late sixties and early seventies, when the country was experiencing social unrest caused by opposition to the war in Vietnam; race riots in Los Angeles, Newark, and Detroit; and growing awareness of environmental degradation. Mitchell was a keen observer of these trends. He joined the Young Presidents' Organization (YPO), a networking club for young CEOs, presidents, and other company heads, and took part in several of its educational tours. He later remarked: "Of all the engineering and professional organizations I belonged to this was the most important one of all."[11] Mitchell valued the group because members talked not only about common business interests but also devoted equal time to learning about emerging social issues. In 1965 Mitchell traveled with the YPO to New York. He tells of meeting some African Americans who had Harvard degrees but because of racial discrimination could not get a bank loan to start a business. The next year the YPO group saw firsthand the destruction in Watts, a neighborhood in Los Angeles that had experienced violent riot-ing. What he saw helped him decide to build a city from scratch: "We went to Watts and saw the destruction of Los Angeles. And I made the decision at that time: we can do a better job in developing our cities. What's happened around the country, Philadelphia, Washington, Baltimore, and all of them, the affluent [citizens] would leave the city and leave the disadvantaged to try to manage the city, which they couldn't do.... We could do a better job. So that was the concept of The Woodlands to begin with."[12]

Mitchell started by studying urban renewal. He and his associates visited new communities in the United States and Europe—England, Sweden, Finland. Houston was growing rapidly at the time. After studying the issues, Mitchell decided to build a town that would have homes for people of different income levels, be environmentally friendly, and offer jobs within the new community. He did not want another suburban development but a whole community.

In the late 1960s, over the course of four years, he bought more than three hundred undeveloped forest tracts north of Houston. Location was important. Most of Houston's growth had been to the south and southwest, where NASA was located and many engineering firms had followed. Houston's real estate experts saw little potential for growth in the north. They strongly advised against developing an entire new community. Mitchell disagreed. In his view, the northwest was Houston's growth corridor. The new international airport was being built at the time—a $3 billion megaproject. The airport, only a half hour by car from his land, would trigger growth for decades to come. Eventually, Mitchell assembled 28,000 acres, enough to build a city for 130,000 people.

What kind of city would it be? The setting for the community was beautiful—dense pine forests and wetlands that Cynthia Mitchell, George's wife, aptly named The Woodlands. Cabell Brand, a businessman who had become a friend of Mitchell on trips with the Young Presidents' Organization, vividly recalls Mitchell's interest in preserving the environment of the new community: "The first thing I'm gonna do is map out the wildlife trails on the land I bought so that we don't mess up the wildlife in the city we're building.... We're going to build a lot of buildings, but we're never going to build anything higher than the trees."[13]

An MND staff member, Robert Hartsfield, remembers that from the very beginning "George intuitively had a feel for nature and what was then beginning to be called environmental planning.... What I did was make it explicit."[14] Hartsfield asked Mitchell to read a just-published book by his college professor, Ian McHarg, called *Design with Nature*.[15] McHarg was chair of the landscape and regional planning department at the University of Pennsylvania and partner in a flourishing consulting firm. He had revolutionized the field of regional planning with his course "Man in the Environment," which he had taught since 1957. Hartsfield saw him as "the father of the environmental planning movement in not only the United States but really the world."[16] McHarg argued for the central role of land in design and refused "to accept that landscape architecture should be subservient to architecture or engineering."[17] Among McHarg's most important projects are the 1962 Plan for the Valleys in Baltimore County, Maryland, the Inner Harbor in Baltimore, and The Woodlands near Houston.

Mitchell was impressed by *Design with Nature*. He contacted the author and hired him to help plan the new town. Two years before construction began McHarg and a team of ten scientists prepared an environmental master plan that set the goal of preserving 25 percent of the original vegetation. They took aerial photographs of the entire area to prepare an inventory of the tree population. Today, the major roads in The Woodlands are lined by seventy-five-foot-wide green belts, and driving on the main thoroughfares, one sees trees, not buildings. In addition, a detailed hydrological study laid the groundwork for flood protection, which is a major concern in the Houston area. While such studies were rarely done at the time, they have since become standard practice for large developments. The U.S. Department of Housing and Urban Development used the Woodlands approach to mandate impact studies as a condition for new communities to receive help from the government.

McHarg's design to use existing vegetation and hydrological patterns to create a sound and esthetically pleasing urban ecology earned The Woodlands the 1993 Prix d'Excellence from the Paris-based International Real Estate Federation—just one of several awards recognizing the high environmental quality of The Woodlands.

The new community differed fundamentally from suburban developments in that a maximum amount of native vegetation was preserved, landscaping and architectural guidelines combined to create an attractive environment, commercial clusters provided a central meeting place for each of six villages, people of different income levels were welcome, gated subdivisions were banned, and the ever-present threat of flooding was contained through imaginative landscaping features, such as using golf courses as temporary holding ponds and allowing street runoff to water lawns. An extensive network of bicycle and pedestrian paths was built that was used mostly for recreation.

Initially development of The Woodlands severely drained the resources of the energy company. Mitchell came close to disaster when the Texas real estate market collapsed during the late seventies and early eighties. Eventually he prevailed. Once oil and gas prices had recovered, Mitchell repaid the banks and released the federal government from a $50 million loan guarantee that he had obtained. Working with the Department of Housing and Urban Development had been an administrative nightmare, but without the federal loan guarantee The Woodlands would not have been built. Thirteen "New Cities," in addition to The Woodlands, received similar loan guarantees from the government. In the end, only The Woodlands did not require a federal subsidy.

In the nineties, The Woodlands began to prosper, and by the turn of the century the city had 80,000 inhabitants. With current growth trends it will take another generation to reach the planned size of 130,000 people. Mitchell's successful lobbying for regional infrastructure improvements, such as the initially controversial toll road from The Woodlands to Houston's Intercontinental Airport and downtown,[18] helped bring about commercial success. Over the years a consensus emerged that the environmentally friendly design of The Woodlands was the single most important factor in this success. A scholarly account of the planning and early development years of The Woodlands was published in 1987.[19] At that time the long-term future of the new community was still uncertain. Even so, the authors concluded that "the Woodlands has prospered—albeit to a lesser degree than expected—because of the superior financial resources of its developer, its favorable location, and the developer's steadfast commitment to the goals and principles of the new-community program."

The new community was designed with respect for nature. It reserved 5 percent of its housing for low-income residents and provided a rising number of jobs close to where people live. Yet two problems must be mentioned: fewer houses for low-income residents have been built than initially envisioned by Mitchell after his visit to Watts, and dependence on private transportation is as dominant as anywhere in the Houston region. There is a good park-and-ride system for those working in downtown Houston, but there is no public transportation in The Woodlands itself.

In 1997, in the early stages of a real estate boom, Mitchell reluctantly followed the recommendation of the MND board of directors and sold The Woodlands for $543 million. The new owners followed most of the design standards that Mitchell had set. But they allowed gated subdivisions, something Cynthia Mitchell had opposed. Environmental standards in newly developed parts of The Woodlands have also been relaxed.[20] In 2003 the Rouse Company, the developer of Columbia, Maryland, bought The Woodlands. Rouse, in turn, was sold to General Growth Properties in 2004.

Planning and building The Woodlands was significant in the context of Mitchell's work on sustainability. It showed his respect for nature and concern for social integration. It also perfectly illustrated how he works. He starts with educating himself about an issue that interests him. He reads widely about it, studies best practices being used worldwide, pays attention to emerging concerns, and then commits the resources that will buy him the best talent available. He used this same approach in promoting sustainability.

Spaceship Earth

Other trips with the Young Presidents' Organization brought Mitchell to the Aspen Institute in Colorado, where he attended seminars on important social and environmental issues. At first, Mitchell lectured on energy at several Aspen Institute meetings. But he, along with many of his business colleagues, was most interested in learning about social issues. He went to Aspen in successive summers from 1968 to 1971. At one of these seminars he met Buckminster Fuller, the mathematician-philosopher who had designed the geodesic dome and coined the phrase "Spaceship Earth." It is this concept— the earth is finite and its resources are limited—that impressed Mitchell deeply and got him started on his long journey on the road to sustainable development. The term "sustainable development" was not yet used at the time. But the basic idea took firm root in Mitchell's mind: Overpopulation is a problem throughout the world, particularly in poor countries. It has negative economic, social, and environmental impacts. Unless these are addressed in a comprehensive and timely manner the conditions for human life on earth will deteriorate, possibly to the point of endangering the survival of the species.

Over the course of three or four days of meetings with Fuller, first listening to his lectures, then meeting with him in a small discussion group, Mitchell

Figure 1. R. Buckminster Fuller, 1895–1983. (Source: United States Postal Service Commemorative Stamp, 2004)

was persuaded of the urgency of the problem. From now on he put it this way: "If you can't make the world work with four billion people [the world population at the time of his meetings with Fuller], how will you manage with six or nine?" From this early beginning and ahead of most contributors to the debate, he was convinced that environmental problems, while important, were but part of a much larger issue—the endangering of natural systems and the resulting threat to human life on earth as we know it.

Fuller's argument was simple: The earth is a spaceship. It has a certain size and capacity and cannot exceed this capacity. The root problem is population growth. From then on Mitchell would repeat this point over and over again: "And if we all don't get our act together in the next 50 or 100 years, we're going to be in deep trouble. Sustainability is a much broader theme than just environmental issues and has to be addressed by all nations as time goes on."[21]

At another Aspen seminar, Mitchell met the British economist E. F. Schumacher, who advocated sustainability—again without yet using the term—through promoting appropriate technology and small projects as a development strategy.[22] Ken Boulding, who brought an ecological perspective to economics, also came to Aspen and discussed common interests with Mitchell. Boulding used to say: "Anyone who believes exponential growth can go on forever in a finite world is either a madman or an economist." In 1966 he published an essay called "The Economics of the Coming Spaceship Earth." The Aspen seminars were a turning point for Mitchell. He could now place his concern about the environment—a concern that had preoccupied him for a number of years—in the much broader context of the future of the world or—as he would soon say—the development of sustainable societies.

CHAPTER 2

The History of Sustainability

The intense debate about sustainability, which started around 1970, has a long history that proceeded in three stages. In 1713 the term first surfaced to denote the sustained yield of a natural resource—wood. Beginning in the nineteenth century, sustainability was defined as the conservation of natural resources. Finally, in 1987, the economic and ecological meanings of sustainability were fused into the now current term sustainable development—a strategy to manage the increasing interdependence between natural and social systems.

Sustained Yield

Ulrich Grober, an independent German scholar, has traced the first use of "sustainability" to 1713, when a book on forestry, *Sylvicultura Oeconomica*, was published in Leipzig.[1] Except for the Latin title, the book is written in German. This massive volume addressed a resource constraint of the time: the increasing scarcity of wood for shoring up mines, building ships, constructing homes, and supplying fuel. The author, Hans Carl von Carlowitz, was a mining administrator. It was part of his job to supply timber to an important mining district in Saxony. He had found this to be difficult. In the book he criticized the rapid transformation of forests into fields where peasants grew cereals and potatoes—the European version of today's destruction of the tropical rain forests. He admitted that agriculture yielded faster profits but argued that deforestation created economic havoc. To increase the supply of wood the author proposed a novel idea: Take agricultural land and plant trees on it. Up to that time trees grew in wild forests, not human-made forests. The book advised the landowner on how to plant trees and, once the forest was mature, how to adopt a cycle of harvesting and restoration that would guarantee a

Figure 2. Cover of Sylvicultura Oeconomica, 1713.

sustainable yield: "daß es eine continuierliche beständige und nachhaltende Nutzung gebe" (that there be a continuous stable and sustainable yield).[2]

The scarcity of wood was overcome in the next few decades, partly by following the author's advice to plant forests, but mostly by substituting coal for wood. The industrial age was about to begin, and coal and iron, rather than wood, became the most coveted natural resources that reshaped European economies. A different approach to the shortage of wood had been used in France when Colbert, the powerful minister of Louis XIV, outlawed deforestation, not to preserve nature but to save the French shipbuilding industry.

Even so, the 1713 treatise on tree cultivation is widely regarded as the first work on scientific forestry.[3] It wielded considerable influence. Throughout the eighteenth and nineteenth centuries forest management in central Europe, primarily on land owned by the nobility, the state, or the church, applied the principle of sustainability. The forest manager was trained never to cut more than the capacity of the forest to grow back. The long time frame of forest growth, decades to a hundred years, forced managers to adopt the concept of intergenerational equity long before it was reintroduced in our time. The classical work on sustainable yield in forest management was published in 1804 by Georg Ludwig Hartig: "There is no continuous forest economy unless the yield of wood is calculated according to the principle of sustainability.... The forest manager must use the forest in such a way that the next generation can benefit at least as much from the forest as the current generation."[4] This passage is strikingly similar to the now famous definition of sustainability in the 1987 United Nations report (see below).

In the twentieth century, the terms "sustained yield" or "safe yield" lived on in technical works on forestry, fisheries, and water management. They were used to describe management techniques that promise sustained harvests over time or a reliable supply of water even under drought conditions. These works cautioned against overfishing, single-species cultivation of forests, or overdrawing water—poor management practices that lead to unsustainable results. Note that the goal is sustained *economic yield*, not protection of the resource, which may happen, but only as a byproduct. In 1960 the U.S. Congress endorsed the sustained yield concept and legislated that it be used in managing the national forests.

Conservation

An entirely different pathway to sustainability came from the work of biologists who studied the relationship between organisms and their environment. In 1866 the German biologist Ernst Haeckel introduced the word *ecology* for this field of study: "Unter Oecologie verstehen wir die gesamte Wissenschaft von den Beziehungen des Organismus zur umgebenden Außenwelt." (By ecology we mean the entire science of the relationships of the organism to the environment.)[5] Haeckel added that these relationships defined the conditions for the existence of life on earth. Ecology was not focused exclusively on the needs of human beings, as was the case of the safe yield approach. Instead, ecology defined sustainability for the entire spectrum of living beings. The Danish biologist Eugen Warming developed Haeckel's concept and is widely regarded as the founder of ecology as a scientific discipline.[6]

Multiple-Use Sustained-Yield Act of 1960
(Public Law 86–517; approved June 12, 1960)

An act to authorize and direct that the national forests be managed under principles of multiple use and to produce a sustained yield of products and services, and for other purposes. … The Secretary of Agriculture is authorized and directed to develop and administer the renewable surface resources of the national forests for multiple use and sustained yield. … "Sustained yield of the several products and services" means the achievement and maintenance in perpetuity of a high level annual or regular periodic output of the various renewable resources of the national forests without impairment of the productivity of the land.

It is only in recent decades that the two meanings—safe yield of a renewable resource and safe conditions for life—merged. It first happened in the context of discussing the need for conserving natural resources. In 1969 the Swiss-based International Union for the Conservation of Nature (IUCN) adopted a new mandate that focused on the "management of air, water, soils, minerals and living species including man, so as to achieve the highest *sustainable* [my italics] quality of life."[7]

Eugen Warming was a Danish botanist and a main founding figure of the scientific discipline of ecology. Warming wrote the first textbook (1895) on plant ecology, taught the first university course in ecology, and gave the concept its meaning and content.

In 1980 the IUCN—by then called the World Conservation Union—further developed this concept. In a joint project with the United Nations Environment Program and the World Wildlife

Fund, IUCN elevated sustainable development to the key strategy for conserving biological resources.[8] The report, *World Conservation Strategy*, identifies these conservation guidelines:

- Use resources in such a way that the resource base is not destroyed;
- Do not interfere with the physical environment to the extent that the conditions for life are endangered;
- Preserve biodiversity, essential ecological processes, and life-support systems;
- Preserve genetic diversity; and
- Use species or ecosystems in a *sustainable manner* [my italics].

The report emphasizes that conservation is not the opposite of development. Instead, conservation is essential for people to achieve a life of dignity and to preserve the welfare of present and future generations. Humanity exists as a part of nature and has no future unless natural resources are conserved. Conservation will not work without development to alleviate the poverty and misery of hundreds of millions of people.

Stressing the interdependence of conservation (nature) and development (society), the World Conservation Union was first to give currency to the term "sustainable development." The 1980 report defined sustainability as the key quality of desirable growth: development that linked the "quality of human life" to the "vitality and diversity of the Earth" (see box). This elevated sustainability above the original economic meaning and focused on the interdependence of natural and social systems. The fundamental new insight was this: There is no human life without functioning natural systems.

Sustainable Development

At the United Nations Conference on the Human Environment in 1972 (the Stockholm Conference), delegates concluded that economic growth and industrialization, goals that so far had eluded the developing countries, could be achieved without damage to the environment. They believed that this was possible if the Third World avoided the mistakes made by the First World during its economic takeoff. But how could they achieve this goal?

To answer this question, in 1982 the General Assembly of the United

Nations convened the World Commission on Environment and Development (WCED). The commission was to formulate "a global agenda for change" and "propose long-term environmental strategies for achieving sustainable development by the year 2000 and beyond." The WCED was chaired by Gro Harlem Brundtland, who had previously served as environment minister and prime minister of Norway and later directed the World Health Organization. William Ruckelshaus was appointed United States commissioner, and Jim MacNeill, a Canadian, served as secretary general. The commission issued its report, *Our Common Future*, in 1987.[9] MacNeill was the principal author. Expanding on his previous work as director for the environment at the Paris-based Organization for Economic Cooperation and Development (OECD), he argued that economy and environment can reinforce each other. Also known as the "Brundtland Report," it noted the various problems of the 1980s, among them environmental accidents in Chernobyl and Bhopal, drought in the Sahel, international trade in hazardous wastes, global warming, and ozone depletion. The report then recommended that a new approach called "sustainable development" be adopted as a global strategy to address environmental and economic issues.

Sustainability

Using renewable natural resources sustainably means doing so in such a way that does not threaten a species by overuse, yet it will optimize benefits to both the environment and human needs. Sustainably using natural resources, including plants, forests, fish, and other wildlife, is an important conservation tool when addressing the increasing pressures on nature by people.

—From the Web site of the World Conservation Union (IUCN)

Sustainable Development

This is a kind of development that provides real improvements in the quality of human life and at the same time conserves the vitality and diversity of the Earth. The goal is development that will be sustainable. Today it may seem visionary but it is attainable.

—IUCN, *World Conservation Strategy*, 1980

Our Common Future set three goals for sustainable development: (1) making growth ecologically responsible, (2) respecting the needs of future generations, and (3) finding a better balance between economic efficiency and social equity. The report's most frequently quoted definition of sustainable development highlights the need for intergenerational equity; in other words, shifting investment and policy decisions from a short-term to a long-term

Figure 3. Cover of *Our Common Future*, 1987.

focus: "Sustainable development is development that meets the needs of the present without compromising the ability of future generations to meet their own needs."

A second quote from the Brundtland Report calls for respect of the nature-society connection: "At a minimum, sustainable development must not endanger the natural systems that support life on Earth: the atmosphere, the waters, the soils, and the living beings." In a less populated world, many of these linkages had been ignored without dire consequences. But the new world of 6 billion people, or 9 billion by the middle of the twenty-first century, must take resource limitations and the health of natural systems seriously and integrate them into policies for jobs, food, energy, water, and transportation.

What is the difference between sustainable development and economic development? The traditional way to define and measure economic growth considers three factors: production, savings, and labor supply. Robert Solow, a Nobel Prize winner, added technological innovation and knowledge. The United Nations' Human Development Index further broadened the concept by including life expectancy, educational attainment, and adjusted real income per person. Ecological economics, a discipline developed by scholars like Kenneth Boulding, Robert Costanza, and Herman Daly, addresses the interdependence between human economies and natural systems. Sustainable development combines all of these elements. Its three "interdependent and mutually reinforcing pillars" are economic development, social development, and environmental protection.[10] This makes it a richer but also less rigorous, and difficult to measure, concept than economic development.

Our Common Future called for broad policy changes at national and international levels: "The world must quickly design strategies that will allow nations to move from their present, often destructive, processes of growth and development onto sustainable development paths."[11]

The UN report had worldwide impact. Interest in sustainable development

---

Policies for Sustainable Development

- Reviving growth
- Changing the quality of growth
- Meeting essential needs for jobs, food, energy, water, and sanitation
- Ensuring a sustainable level of population
- Conserving and enhancing the resource base
- Reorienting technology and managing risk
- Merging environment and economics in decision making

—WCED, *Our Common Future*, p. 49

increased dramatically, both in developed and developing countries. In the years following the report's publication, innumerable books and papers tried to further develop and apply the concept of sustainability. Many conferences, including the World Summits convened by the United Nations in Rio de Janeiro and Johannesburg, were devoted to the same goal. Detailed guidelines for implementing the principles of sustainability in a wide range of economic and social activities were approved at the UN conference in Rio de Janeiro as *Agenda 21*.[12] The Rio declaration, passed at the same conference, affirmed the concept of sustainable development for the world community.

In practical terms, progress toward the goals in the declaration has been slow, reflecting the preference of voters and policy makers for narrowly defined short-term solutions.

But the concept of sustainable development remains a powerful model for thinking about the future of human society. Proponents hope that attention to sustainability will improve on earlier concepts of development in two important respects. First, it will link the economic, ecological, and social spheres of human activities and thereby offer societies an integrated way to deal with the complexity of modern life. Second, sustainable development considers long-term impacts and outcomes and thereby goes beyond the immediate future. But success in the world of ideas has created its own problems. The concept of sustainable development has become so popular that it often loses focus as more and more groups and causes claim that sustainability expresses their vastly different interests.

"Sustainable development" has become overused, unclear, and almost unhelpful. Perhaps it is now time to reconceptualize and rename "sustainable development" to encompass the additional issues that have been raised at Club of Rome conferences and elsewhere. It needs to include sustainable human development and sustainable livelihood.

—From a report on the 1999 conference of the Club of Rome

At the same time no other concept has emerged that captures the triple challenge of our time: sustainable yield of renewable resources, protection of ecosystems, and reduction of poverty. Each of these three pillars of sustainability remains important.

George Mitchell read *Our Common Future* and called it "a good report." While it was being prepared he met several times with Ruckelshaus, the American commissioner. In 1985, after discussions with the secretary general of the commission, the Mitchell Center (see chapter 7) offered its services as the U.S. office of the American commissioner. Ruckelshaus liked the idea but in the end nothing came of the proposal.

William Ruckelshaus, in Mitchell's view, was "really for environmental issues and sustainability." Even so, Mitchell believed that except for statements and conferences, the UN strategy "never went anywhere."[13] This is the perception shared by many, although this criticism ignores the impact the report had. *Our Common Future* changed the mindset of people. Organizations in Third World countries in particular embraced the ideas presented in the report. Here, for the first time, was a strategy that industrialized and developing countries could share, both working for similar goals but with different roles. This was a great accomplishment at a time when the world was still split between Western, Communist, and Third World economies. Over the last twenty years the concept of sustainable development has changed the work of international agencies such as the World Bank and innumerable nongovernmental organizations throughout the world. Its biggest impact to date may well be at the local and regional levels, where small institutions eagerly espoused the new development strategy. National governments, as well as many international organizations, have been more reluctant to change their policies and programs.

CHAPTER 3

The Need for Sustainable Development

Why does the world need sustainable development more urgently to-day than in previous times? Answering this question requires a look back in time. I begin with a remark made by my favorite college professor that I never forgot. He wanted us to understand that social and economic change occurs at different speeds in human history. To illustrate the point he compared living conditions at the time of the American and French revolutions with those during the Roman era. In his view, Washington and Napoleon lived in a world closer to Caesar and Augustus than to Kennedy and De Gaulle. A chronological distance of eighteen hundred years had brought less change in human affairs than the last two hundred years. As evidence, my teacher pointed to agriculture, transportation, and human life expectancy. By 1800 these had not changed much since Roman days. Agriculture still provided the livelihood of most people. Transportation was still by horse, and nobody had built better roads than the Romans. The average life span remained at under forty years. All this changed dramatically over the course of the next two hundred years. During this short time span, humankind made unprecedented social progress but also put in place the ingredients for serious threats to our commons.

Population Growth

Two factors account for the accelerated pace of change since 1800: population growth and technological innovation. They are closely intertwined. In 1800, 1 billion people lived on earth (see Figure 4). It had taken thousands of years and the inventions of tool making, agriculture, and writing, to reach this level. But from then on the world population grew at much faster rates, reaching 2 billion in 1927, 4 billion in 1974, and 6.5 billion in 2006.[1] The doubling

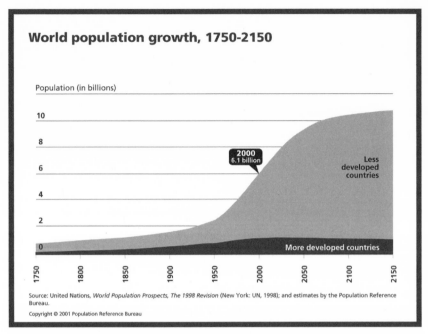

Figure 4. World population growth, 1750–2150. (Source: United Nations, *World Population Prospects: The 1998 Revision* [New York: United Nations, 1998]; and estimates by the Population Reference Bureau. Copyright © 2001 Population Reference Bureau.)

time shrank from 130 to 50 and now 30 years. Demographers explain the population explosion of the last two centuries as the product of economic growth, increased income levels, improved nutrition, and better health care. All of this is eminently desirable on a personal level, but in the aggregate it has caused unforeseen problems that damage social and natural systems. In 1970, when the world counted "only" 3.5 billion people, Paul and Anne Ehrlich issued this stark warning: "No geological event in a billion years—not the emergence of mighty mountain ranges, nor the submergence of entire subcontinents, nor the occurrence of periodic glacial ages—has posed a threat to terrestrial life comparable to that of human overpopulation."[2]

What about the future? Demographers predict that by 2150 the world population will reach 9.5 to 10.5 billion people. This number is lower than projections made several decades ago, when experts expected that continued high fertility, combined with declining death rates, might result in a 2150 population between 14 and 16 billion. Today we can say with confidence that the world population will peak by 2150 and then begin a gradual decline. Ninety-five percent of the increase will have occurred by 2050.

To put these numbers in perspective, consider these facts:

1. The rate of population growth between 1800 and 2050 is unprecedented in human history.
2. People older than forty-five years have witnessed the doubling of world population within their lifetime. This had never happened before.
3. The population explosion is being halted by declining poverty and by voluntary decisions by couples, in particular those living in cities, to limit the number of children they have. Unlike in earlier times, population is not being controlled by famine, disease, or natural disasters.
4. In 1950 the ratio of people living in developed compared to developing countries was 1:2; in 2050 it will be 1:6.[3]

Peter Vitousek and his coauthors have summarized the multiple novel changes that the rising human population is causing to the world's ecosystems. The authors conclude: "Human alteration of Earth is substantial and growing.... We are changing Earth more rapidly than we are understanding it."[4] The most critical time for understanding as well as action will be in the next few decades. This is a short time span. Today's children will have to provide food, water, energy, and jobs for an additional 3 to 4 billion people, most of them living in the mega cities of developing countries. At the same time they must develop, test, and apply strategies for reaching two additional goals: protect nature and reduce poverty. The nations of the world provided food, shelter, and energy for most of the 3 billion new people that were born between 1970 and today. But during those four decades the world made only limited progress in protecting nature and lifting people out of poverty. Therefore, the lessons learned and policies implemented during the last forty years are not a sufficient blueprint for the next forty years.

How many people can the earth support? This is an age-old question. Babylonian cuneiform tablets tell the story of how the gods were annoyed about the earth filling up with ever more people who made so much noise that they deprived them of sleep. So the gods sent disasters to reduce the number of people—plague, drought, famine, and finally the big flood. When the waters had receded the gods told the Babylonian Noah that henceforth not all women would bear children and some children would never be born. The biblical Noah received a different message: "Be fruitful and multiply and fill the earth." In Babylon's scarce fertile land between the Euphrates and Tigris rivers, people feared overpopulation, but the people of biblical Israel were eager to grow in number.[5]

Three thousand years later, in 1798, Thomas Malthus predicted famine unless people followed the iron rule "that population must always be kept down to the level of the means of subsistence."[6] Recurrent periods of famine seemed to support his warning. In the nineteenth century millions of people escaped the threat of famine by leaving crowded Europe to cultivate new lands in America, Africa, and Australia. This strategy worked for them but destroyed the livelihoods of indigenous people such as Native Americans and Australian aborigines.

Eventually, technology came to the rescue. Chemical fertilizers, widespread irrigation, new crop varieties, and modern farming techniques increased food production worldwide. The "green revolution," supported by the Rockefeller Foundation, developed in Mexico, and fully applied in India, used seeds with improved genetic qualities to increase yield and end famine in many parts of the world.[7] This is just one recent instance of the link between technological innovation and population growth. To understand this relentless dynamic, with its good as well as bad results, we need to look more closely at technological change.

More on Population Growth

Look for historical and projected population data at the Web sites of the United Nations Population Bureau (www.un.org/esa/population/unpop.htm) and the Washington-based Population Reference Bureau (www.prb.org).

Joel E. Cohen, *How Many People Can the Earth Support?* (New York: W. W. Norton, 1995)

Paul R. Ehrlich, *The Population Bomb* (New York: Ballantine, 1968). This book brought the population problem to the attention of a wide audience.

Massimo Livi-Bacci, *A Concise History of World Population: An Introduction to Population Processes,* 3rd edition (Oxford: Blackwell, 2001)

Michael Balter, "The Baby Deficit," *Science* 312 (June 30, 2006): 1894–97

Technological Change

Population growth accelerated dramatically after 1800 mainly because of an unprecedented increase in economic productivity made possible by innovations in technology, science, and management, which brought wealth and health as well as unforeseen social and environmental problems.[8] The links in this long chain of events are four waves of industrial revolution.

First Industrial Revolution

The first industrial revolution—in our schoolbooks we read about it as *the* industrial revolution—lasted from 1760 to 1860.[9] Britain led the way by mastering the new technologies of textile manufacturing, iron making, steam power, railroads, banking, and insurance.[10] These new industries gave Britain the strength to checkmate Napoleon's attempt to rule Europe and then to embark on her own quest for world empire. British society and government encouraged trade and commerce. The strong parliamentary system exercised little control over the economy but created a political environment friendly to private entrepreneurship. A recent study traces Britain's advantage over continental European countries to two critical factors: high wages and cheap coal. Manpower was expensive while machine power was cheap.[11] This encouraged innovation aimed at the substitution of labor by machines. The new industrial system brought factories, mill towns, large cities, urban slums, trade unions, modern political parties, and new economic and social policies. Industrial development generated wealth, but it also created a large urban workforce that suffered from miserable working conditions. The novels of Charles Dickens offer a vivid picture of that new world and the plight of the working poor in nineteenth-century England. Passage of the revolutionary Poor Laws of the 1830s started the world on the road to governmental welfare policies. By 1850 every aspect of Britain's social and economic life had been changed by the industrial revolution.

Industrialization in continental Europe followed the British model after a delay of several decades. When it happened, the social and economic problems caused by the transition from agriculture to industry were even more intense, including labor unrest, revolutions, and massive changes in public institutions and policies. The downside of industrialization in Western Europe comes to life in the novels of Emile Zola.

Second Industrial Revolution

During the *second industrial revolution*, from about 1860 to 1960, first Germany and then the United States took over technological and economic leadership. The key technologies and industries, many of them still important in today's economies, were steel, electricity, synthetic chemicals, the internal combustion engine, and communications by telegraph and telephone. Two managerial inventions changed the way an advanced industrial society works. First, the assembly line made possible the mass production of consumer goods. This was an entirely American invention.[12] It enabled the United States to build a powerful national economy, become an affluent society, and claim world leadership. The assembly line relied on the carefully planned division of labor among workers and the use of interchangeable parts. One of its many consequences was a revolution in industrial architecture and urban land use. Factories were no longer multistory buildings, but large horizontal plants where raw materials entered on one side and finished products came out on the other. The increased space requirements for manufacturing plants, combined with new means of transportation, made it cheaper for industry to locate outside the heart of large cities. Over time, this led to the decline of inner cities and the development of suburbia.

The second managerial innovation during this period was organized research and development. It emerged in the middle of the nineteenth century in Germany, but the United States quickly recognized its importance. The main components of organized research were specialized laboratories, precise scientific instruments, a research team with senior and apprentice scientists, a resource base, and a client. This way of conducting research spawned two new institutions: the research university and the industrial research division. German universities developed the model and led research in many fields of science until 1933. Companies like Badische Anilin und Soda Fabrik (BASF) invented chemical fertilizers and synthetic dyes.

In America, Johns Hopkins University, established in 1876, was first to place research at the center of graduate training. Other universities followed rapidly and relied on private donors and industry rather than government to support the new way of operating. General Electric (GE), American Telephone and Telegraph (AT&T), and DuPont built world-famous research divisions. Discoveries in organic chemistry created science-based industries, first synthetic dyes and fertilizers, and later pharmaceutical drugs and plastics.

Science previously had focused on producing theoretical knowledge; now it spawned technological innovations, and the two together—science plus engineering—became the engine of economic development.

Modern production techniques and the science-technology-production link brought about massive social changes. Industrial centers grew into large metropolitan agglomerations. The development of national systems of transportation and communication elevated economic operations from regional to national levels. Industry and labor became powerful political forces. Agriculture lost its dominant place in society. The political agenda was recast in response to the new conditions.

Two new policy needs were addressed. First, the sheer power of industry needed to be tamed: How could a strong national economy be built without letting industry run the country? The second concern was with the worker and his family: How would society protect the worker from the risks associated with work in industry, such as unemployment, occupational disease, and industrial accidents? And how would workers and their families be provided for in old age and illness? Different nations tried different solutions, leading to modern capitalism, socialism, and communism. In the United States, from the 1880s to the Great Depression of the 1930s, the main policy goal was to control corporate mergers, trusts, and monopolies. During the New Deal, priorities shifted to regulation of financial operations, labor relations, and social security. The foundations of the American version of the welfare state were laid at this time.

By 1960 the Western nations had fully developed their policy response to the second industrial revolution. While there were vast differences in detail, each nation relied on three main strategies. First, in economic policy national governments were now confident that they could smooth, by means of financial controls and public spending, the cycles of growth and recession. Second, in social policy, governments underwrote, in the interest of equity and justice, large investments in welfare programs designed to meet the special needs of the working population as well as those that were too old or too sick to work. Third, to encourage continued technological innovation, countries created a science policy system that funded research and development in support of defense, health, and economic development. In sum, government policies were now focused on economic and social measures to regulate industrial growth and power and to solve the "social question," as Karl Marx had called the downside of the industrial revolution. Environmental issues, such as water and air pollution, were present but, with few exceptions, were tolerated as the price of progress.

Third Industrial Revolution and Beyond

Priorities changed in the 1960s. Concerns about the safety, health, and environmental side effects of industrial operations became prominent after scientists found evidence of the dangers posed by pollutants in air and water, pesticides, and toxic chemicals. The *third industrial revolution*, which started at this time, is characterized by responding to these environmental problems and by the emergence of ground-breaking science-based technologies and industries. What had begun with the case of synthetic chemicals—the marriage between fundamental research and technological applications—became the norm. Nuclear energy, microelectronics, informatics, and biotechnology sprang entirely from basic scientific research. These industries have by now spread to all parts of the world and have helped most countries to embark on a rapid path to economic development and improved living standards.

Powerful technologies and their global applications have caused multiple social and environmental side effects, today's equivalent of the "social question" produced by the first and second industrial revolutions. We call them environmental problems. But they are more than that. More people, ever higher levels of consumption in the West, and the spread of Western-style industrialization to the farthest corners of the globe are the root causes of resource depletion, pollution, and other injuries to natural and social systems. The list of threats is long: pollution of air, land, and water; poisoning by toxic substances; exhaustion of natural resources; loss of biodiversity; depletion of the ozone layer; acidification of lakes and soils, and global climate change. Each of these problems has a direct connection to the increasing number of human beings living on earth and the powerful technologies invented by them to provide for their needs and luxuries.

The search for solutions has spawned new environmental policies to control pollution, regulate toxic substances, protect the ozone layer, preserve endangered species, reduce acid rain, and control greenhouse gas emissions. There has been progress in dealing with some, but not all, of these problems. Starting in the late 1960s, the world began to recognize that environmental problems were just one manifestation of the effects of growth. Resource constraints—food, water, energy—might endanger all economic, social, and political systems. The damage to natural systems could be severe, disturbing nature's life-support systems and threatening the living conditions of plants and animals, including the human species. This insight is at the heart of today's debate about sustainability.

The outlines of the fourth industrial revolution are now becoming visible. A key driver for change is climate change—in the view of most scientists a consequence of growth and innovation—that is rapidly making itself felt, earlier than experts had predicted only a few years ago. To avoid unmanageable consequences of climate change, the world must build an economy that is less dependent on fossil fuels. The fourth industrial revolution will strive for increased energy efficiency and a gradual shift to nonfossil sources of energy— wind, solar, biofuels, algae, clean coal, and, perhaps, advanced nuclear energy. Information technology, nanotechnology, and biotechnology will revolutionize production and consumption. Advanced materials will be lighter and their production will require less energy input. Many of these emerging technologies are not yet ready or are too expensive for market penetration. At this time the outcome of the race between unacceptable levels of global warming and a decarbonized economy is undecided. But incentives for moving in this direction are growing stronger by the day. The new economy, if it can be developed in time, will make the decisive step toward sustainability.

CHAPTER 4

The Club of Rome

Following his meetings at the Aspen Institute with Buckminster Fuller, E. F. Schumacher, and Ken Boulding, George Mitchell began to read about growth and resource limitations. He shared his thoughts with his wife, Cynthia. The Mitchell children told me that their mother influenced many of Mitchell's decisions, in particular those related to nature and the environment. The two Mitchells agreed that resource depletion, urbanization, environmental degradation, and explosive population growth were threatening the planet and very little was being done to alter these trends. George began to act in 1973 after he learned about the Club of Rome and its first report, *The Limits to Growth*. The work of the Club of Rome moved him from thinking to action. It was a milestone for him, as it was for the entire sustainable development movement that began to take shape at this time.

The Club of Rome, founded in 1968, is the first organization in the world that raised fundamental questions about overpopulation and overconsumption. Its founders were Alexander King, a Scottish scientist, and Aurelio Peccei, an Italian businessman. They formed an unlikely alliance that had worldwide impact. King described their twosome in these terms: "Aurelio, an exuberant Latin industrialist with an economics background, and I, a quiet Scotsman, international civil servant and scientist."[1]

Alexander King was trained as a chemist at the Imperial College in London and the University of Munich. In 1939 he was hired by Sir Henry Tizzard, science adviser to the British prime minister, to help mobilize science for the war. King identified DDT as an important insecticide and organized its production, thus helping Britain to control malaria in the Pacific war theater. In 1942 the British government sent him to Washington to brief American scientists about the development of nuclear weapons. He served there as scientific attaché until 1947, concerned with, as he once said, "everything from penicillin to the bomb." Back in England he worked as chief scientist at the Department of Scientific and Industrial Research. In 1957 he moved to Paris, where he became director of scientific affairs at the Marshall Plan agency for the reconstruction of Europe, today called the Organization for Economic Cooperation and Development (OECD)—an influential think tank of the industrialized nations.[2]

By the early sixties, King had assembled a team of eager young men and women (I was one of them) to work on projects designed to link science to social and economic development. King saw science and technology as engines of progress and advocated a more deliberate use of science and technology in policy making and implementation. But he also recognized the need for government intervention to prevent technology from causing environmental damage. At the time, environmental protection was not high on the agenda of OECD member countries. Following the destruction wrought by World War II they sought economic growth at almost any price. This would change a few years later. In the meantime King looked for opportunities to pursue his environmental ideas in an institutional setting that was more permissive than that of a formal international organization. With his ability to circulate freely among scientists, businessmen, and government officials he was well prepared to informally bring together members of these different communities. He was able to capitalize on this skill after a chance encounter with Aurelio Peccei.

Aurelio Peccei had been trained as an economist and now managed a large Italian consulting firm. Before the war he had run the Fiat division in China; after the war he did the same in Latin America. Then he rebuilt Olivetti, a large Italian office-machine company that had run into difficulties. By the 1960s this successful industrialist had grown increasingly concerned about the future of humankind, the topic of his book *The Chasm Ahead* (1969).

When they met, Peccei and King discovered common ground. They both sought answers to some fundamental questions: Was the world growing too fast? Would it permanently be split between rich and poor nations? Was humanity running out of natural resources? Did society have the tools to deal with environmental problems? Peccei wrote: "Alex King and I were at once on the same wavelength.... He is passionately concerned with the interrelatedness of technical, economic, human and ethical elements of society."[3]

King's assessment of Peccei was equally warm. Upon their first meeting in Paris, "we talked at length and quickly established a bond that lasted until his death in 1984."[4]

In April 1968 the two men convened thirty individuals from ten countries in Rome to discuss, as they put it, "the current and future predicament of man." The predicament, in their view, was that new "global threats such as overpopulation, environmental degradation, poverty and misuse of technology ... did not seem to be attracting sufficient recognition, nor did there seem to be any single body capable of analyzing, let alone starting, significant action against them."[5]

The meeting was a complete failure, mainly because the European participants disliked the discussion paper that King's assistant had prepared. The paper emphasized American systems analysis as a tool for studying complex issues. Attendees also found it difficult to agonize about problems that seemed to lie in the distant future. A smaller meeting in Peccei's home followed. Out of this meeting grew the Club of Rome—an invisible college in the tradition of the Lunar Society in Birmingham whose members, as King often told us, had predicted that science and technology would play a critically important role in the coming industrial age. The Club of Rome was to have no more than one hundred like-minded members from all five continents and sectors of society. It was organized as an informal association that would keep its independence by operating on a small budget and without ever accepting government funding.[6] The goal was "to understand the varied but interdependent components—economic, political, natural and social—that make up the global system in which we all live; to bring that new understanding to the attention of policy-makers and the public worldwide; and in this way to promote new policy initiatives and action."[7]

Mission of the Club of Rome

- To adopt a global approach to the vast and complex problems of a world in which interdependence is increasingly close between the nations within a single planetary system;
- Seeking a deeper understanding of the interactions within the tangle of contemporary problems—political, economic, social, cultural, psychological, technological, and environmental—for which the Club has coined the phrase "the world problematique";
- Focus on long-term perspectives and issues which will determine the lot of future generations.

—From the Club of Rome brochure, 1984

Limits to Growth

By 1970 the Club of Rome had initiated its first project. Dennis L. Meadows, a young systems analyst at the Massachusetts Institute of Technology, was commissioned to prepare a report "on the predicament of mankind." Financial support had been secured from the Volkswagen Foundation. Meadows and the sixteen-member expert team he assembled decided to study five factors that impact growth—population, food production, use of natural resources, industrial production, and pollution. Instead of examining each issue separately, the all-important linkages between them were analyzed with the help of a computer model of the world's economy and physical resources. The model had been developed by specialists in system dynamics, led by Jay Forrester, Meadows' boss at MIT.[8] This had never been tried before. When Forrester presented his World3 model to the executive committee of the Club of Rome, led by King and Peccei, he proposed to make the model the cornerstone of the first Club of Rome project. The committee agreed. Forrester was the intellectual father of *The Limits to Growth;* Dennis Meadows the team director; and Donella Meadows the principal author.

Society "has long bought the idea of continual growth in population and production without adding up the final reckoning. Now a team of MIT scientists, with the aid of a giant computer, has completed a study of the future if present growth continues. Their inescapable conclusions are beyond anyone's grimmest fears. Possibly within as little as 70 years, our social and economic system will collapse unless drastic changes are made very soon."

—From *The Limits to Growth* (1972), back cover of the paperback edition

The results of the Meadows study were first presented at the Smithsonian Institution in Washington, D.C., on March 12, 1972. Dennis Meadows recalls: "The room was packed. Ambassadors, congressmen, senior corporate officials ... were there, standing room only, to hear the results."[9] The book that summarized the findings, *The Limits to Growth*, was published in the same year. It grew out of a brief that Donella Meadows had written for the executive committee of the Club of Rome, whose members had found it difficult to follow the technical papers prepared by the Meadows team. The book sold over 20 million copies and was translated into thirty languages. The *New York Times* called it "one of the most important documents of our age." The Club of Rome members as well as the authors were stunned by the impact of this

THE LIMITS TO growth

Donella H. Meadows
Dennis L. Meadows
Jørgen Randers
William W. Behrens III

A Report for THE CLUB OF ROME'S Project on the
Predicament of Mankind

 A POTOMAC ASSOCIATES BOOK $ 2.75

Figure 5. Cover of *The Limits to Growth*, 1972.

abridged version. The full report was published in two technical volumes, which found few readers.[10] As in the case of Rachel Carson's book, *Silent Spring*, the reader-friendly presentation of *Limits to Growth* was as important as the substance of the study.

Peccei and King found their highest expectations met: "If the Club of Rome has any merit," said Peccei, "it is that of having been the first to rebel against the suicidal ignorance of the human condition."[11]

Peccei and his colleagues presented the study results at the highest levels, including meetings with heads of states or prime ministers in Austria, Germany, and Mexico. The world took notice—but

> Mark this book. It may be as important to mankind as the Council of Nicaea and Martin Luther's 95 Theses. It is a revolutionary new way of looking at man and society.
> —*National Observer*

soon turned its attention to more immediate concerns. King and Peccei realized that governments needed to respond to short-term and pressing local issues. They hoped, however, that this would change once the Club of Rome, and similar initiatives, had been successful in fully informing voting citizens of this global crisis.

The message of *The Limits to Growth* was a stark warning: Population, use of minerals, demands for food and energy, as well as environmental pollution were growing exponentially. This was unsustainable. The problem was not that resources would be fully depleted but that the capital cost of producing them would rise to astronomical levels. Unless growth was curbed, this dynamic would lead to economic and social decline, possibly collapse, within decades. An "equilibrium state sustainable far into the future"[12] was attainable but would require changes in technology and social values in addition to limiting growth. The changes considered in the computer model included resource recycling, pollution control, increased "lifetime of capital," restoration of depleted soil, and increased emphasis on providing food and services rather than on industrial production.

Figure 6, "Arable Land," illustrates the approach used by the Meadows team. Throughout the world the total area available for agriculture was calculated at 3.2 billion hectares. Half of this area was used for agriculture in 1970. Even if the world's people decided to pay the high capital cost of developing the remaining half, they would lose the race against rapidly rising population

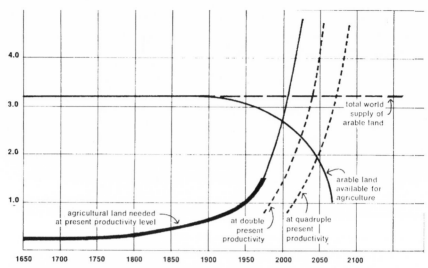

Figure 6. Arable land. (Source: *The Limits to Growth*, p. 60)

numbers. By 2010 the world would no longer have enough land too feed everyone. If agricultural productivity was increased four times, the day of reckoning would come in 2070. In reality, it would come earlier because agricultural land is constantly lost to urbanization and industrialization. When this was factored in, even higher productivity would delay food scarcity only until 2050.

How did the report stand the test of time? Dennis Meadows himself, thirty years after publication of *The Limits to Growth*, was convinced that the study had erred only at the margin. Addressing the Club of Rome in 2004, Meadows said:

> What an enormous shift has occurred in our understanding of the global environment over the past three decades! In the 1970s, before the Club's promotion of *Limits to Growth*, there was little recognition that society could destroy important global systems. Today there is little hope that we can avoid causing profound and permanent damage to natural processes, such as climate regulation and regeneration of marine fisheries. No book has chronicled this shift in perception better than *The Limits to Growth*. The first edition, published in 1972, created an international sensation and acquainted millions with the fact that industrial and population growth could destroy their own foundations—confronting global society

with the very real prospects of collapse. Now a revised edition of the book makes the message relevant for a new century.... The message that current growth trends cannot be sustained is now reconfirmed every year by thousands of headlines, hundreds of conferences, and dozens of new scientific studies. But these focus on specific problems like global warming, soil loss, extinction of species and declining tropical forests. Unfortunately ... all these well intentioned efforts are destined to fail until they are grounded in understanding the complex system governing the causes and consequences of growth in the world's physical economy, materials and energy flows, and population. *Limits to Growth* is so far the only book to provide that understanding.[13]

In my 2007 interview with Meadows, he forcefully stated that small steps—hybrid cars, solar energy, efficient light bulbs—would buy time but in the end would not avert disaster. "Our society is ... so incredibly far away from sustainability that enormous disruptive changes are required and will come, one way or another."[14]

Even though there was criticism of the report (see box), *The Limits to Growth* was a giant step in understanding human societies that grow at a much faster rate than ever experienced before. The report identified critical problem areas and bottlenecks that had remained outside the policy and academic debates. Instead of dealing with each problem separately, the authors applied new computer modeling techniques—the World3 model—to identify linkages and feedbacks among growth factors. *The Limits to Growth* was written with minimal technical jargon, making the book accessible to a large audience.

Still, the report, while highlighting resource and food shortages, failed to foresee the potential for solving the food and other resource supply problems. The vision for a more sustainable future was mentioned: "It is possible to ... establish a condition of ecological and economic stability that is sustainable far into the future."[15] However, not much detail on how to reach this goal was given. It considered industrial pollution but said little about systemic threats to air, land, and water, which in 1972 had not yet attracted the world's attention. Also, the report focused on the industrialized world and said little about the problems of the developing world. The report used then-available demographic knowledge that predicted population growth to reach 14 to 16 billion. This assumption has been proved wrong since then. Due to declining poverty and urbanization, the desired family size has decreased from six to three children, leading to estimates of a world population in the 9 billion range by 2150. This is a major change. Even so, these shortcomings did not invalidate the book's revolutionary contribution to our thinking about the future of human societies in Spaceship Earth.

Blueprint for Survival

In January 1972, just months before *The Limits to Growth* was published, the new British journal *The Ecologist* devoted an entire issue to a discussion of new environmental threats and ways to rescue the planet. The issue addressed much of the same agenda as *The Limits to Growth*, of which the editors had detailed knowledge. The magazine's *A Blueprint for Survival* opened with the following statement:

1. An examination of the relevant information available has impressed upon us the extreme gravity of the global situation today. For, if current trends are allowed to persist, the breakdown of society and the irreversible disruption of the life-support systems on this planet, possibly by the end of the century, certainly within the lifetimes of our children, are inevitable.

2. Governments[,] and ours is no exception, are either refusing to face the relevant facts, or are briefing their scientists in such a way that

---

Criticism of *The Limits to Growth*

Robert M. Solow, an economist from MIT and Nobel Prize winner in 1987, complained about the weak base of data on which *Limits to Growth*'s predictions were made.

Dr. Allen Kneese and Dr. Ronald Riker of Resources for the Future: "The authors load their case by letting some things grow exponentially and others not. Population, capital and pollution grow exponentially in all models, but technologies for expanding resources and controlling pollution are permitted to grow, if at all, only in discrete increments."

The futurist Herman Kahn: "With current and near current technology, we can support 15 billion people in the world ... for a millennium."

The economist Julian Simon: "The material conditions of life will continue to get better for most people, in most countries, most of the time, indefinitely."

—All of the above from *Newsweek,* March 13, 1972, p. 103

Christopher Freeman: "Since ... brute poverty is still a major problem, we do not accept (the MIT team's) enthusiastic endorsement of zero growth as the ideal for the world.... We their seriousness is played down. Whatever the reasons, no corrective measures of any consequence are being undertaken.

3. This situation has already prompted the formation of the Club of Rome, a group of scientists and industrialists from many countries, which is currently trying to persuade governments, industrial leaders and trade unions throughout the world to face these facts and to take appropriate action while there is yet time. It must now give rise to a national movement to act at a national level, and if need be to assume political status and contest the next general election. It is hoped that such an example will be emulated in other countries, thereby giving rise to an international movement, complementing the invaluable work being done by the Club of Rome.

> believe that … the MIT group is underestimating the possibilities of continuous technical progress."
> —From *Models of Doom*, edited by H. S. D. Cole et al. (New York: Universe Books, 1973), p. 10

4. Such a movement cannot hope to succeed unless it has previously formulated a new philosophy of life, whose goals can be achieved without destroying the environment and a precise and comprehensive programme for bringing about the sort of society in which it can be implemented.[16]

In three sections, *A Blueprint for Survival* defined the need for change, recommended a strategy for change, and defined the goal of change—a stable, sustainable society.[17] There was much interest in the publication, and it was published in book form in both England and the United States.[18] While this was the first instance the term "sustainable society" was used to describe a broad goal for humanity's future, the text is difficult to read and no match to the writing and analysis of *The Limits to Growth*.

Mankind at the Turning Point

Two years after publication of *The Limits to Growth*, the second report to the Club of Rome was published. *Mankind at the Turning Point* was structured around the concept of "organic growth."[19] Mihajlo Mesarovic and Eduard Pestel, professors from Cleveland, Ohio, and Hanover, Germany, followed

Figure 7. Cover of *A Blueprint for Survival*, 1972.

Mankind at the Turning Point

By Mihajlo Mesarovic and Eduard Pestel

The Second Report to The Club of Rome

Figure 8. Cover of *Mankind at the Turning Point*, 1974.

the example of the first report and examined critical problem areas, in particular the world food shortage, the energy crisis, population growth, and disparity in economic development. But in contrast to the first report, the authors did not examine these issues at the global scale, an approach that had led to major problems of data availability and aggregation. Instead, the authors divided the world into ten large regions with similar political, economic, and environmental characteristics. This avoided the problem of aggregating data into often meaningless world averages that, in the view of many critics, had weakened the findings of *The Limits to Growth*.

The new report argued that the gap between the rich "North" and the poor "South" was as important as the gap between humans and nature: "Both gaps must be narrowed if world-shattering catastrophes are to be avoided; but they can be narrowed only if global 'unity' and Earth's 'finiteness' are explicitly recognized."[20] Borrowing from the distinction between *organic* (good) and *undifferentiated* (bad) growth in nature, the report calls for consideration of growth in the context of particular world regions: "While undifferentiated growth is assuming truly cancerous qualities in some parts of the world, the very existence of man is threatened daily in some other part by lack of growth; e.g., in regional food production."[21]

The leaders of the Club of Rome, Peccei and King, commented that Mesarovic and Pestel's study, because it recognized regional diversity, was precise enough to guide policy decisions. "For the first time it is now possible, by confronting the policies of different groups competing among themselves within the finite capacity of the planet, to delineate areas of conflict or incompatibility inherent in national or regional policies."[22]

On April 27, 2006, the son of Aurelio Peccei, at a meeting in Washington, D.C., awarded the Lifetime Achievement Award of the Club of Rome to George and Cynthia Mitchell (see Appendix 5).

CHAPTER 5

Early Woodlands Conferences

George Mitchell was impressed by the work of the Club of Rome and its first reports. He felt that Europeans, being from older societies, were far ahead of Americans in paying attention to new problems caused by population growth and resource depletion. In his view, the Club of Rome had accomplished a great deal by starting the debate about growth, consumption, and pollution. Europeans also were less afraid of government intervention that would turn problem recognition into policy.[1] In Mitchell's view *The Limits to Growth* addressed the issues that mattered—population growth, use of nonrenewable resources, increased need for food and energy, and rising levels of pollution. The report went beyond earlier works by providing detailed numbers on past trends and expected future growth. Mitchell called the book "a first wakeup call" about the new threats facing the world.[2] "I read the book *Limits to Growth* by Dennis Meadows and it just impressed the hell out of me. I realized that the book could have all sorts of things wrong with it, but the concept was important."[3]

Mitchell had two reservations, both important. First, small mistakes in using baseline data in the computer model were likely to lead to big mistakes as future growth patterns were calculated. This was a problem he was only too familiar with in the energy business, where projections of remaining resources of oil and gas often turned out to be far from the mark. Second, he disliked the report's recommendation for action: governments should intervene to limit growth. He felt that growing population numbers worldwide, particularly in developing countries, excluded this option, at least as a general prescription for all countries. He much preferred the distinction between good and bad growth that was at the heart of *Mankind at the Turning Point:* "I knew that there had to be limits on some growth, but not limits on other growth."[4] He shared the view that growth was bad when it overtaxed nature—either by using too many nonrenewable natural resources, or by releasing too much waste into air, water, or soil. But growth was good when it used resources efficiently, reduced waste loads, and was directed at meeting essential human needs.

Whatever his reservations about the first report, Mitchell was convinced that the debate started by *The Limits to Growth* was healthy. It needed to be encouraged. He was eager to make this happen in the United States. Always in favor of the direct approach, Mitchell picked up the phone and asked Dennis Meadows how he might help. "I called him on the telephone, and we started discussing things about limited growth, starting ... in 1973. And I mentioned [that] maybe I would organize a conference, and Dennis agreed to be the front leader of it."[5] This led to many visits and long debates between the two men. Mitchell expressed his view that economic growth was needed, at least for as long as population numbers continued to rise. In Mitchell's recollection, Meadows and he "realized that *Limits to Growth* was not the right answer, and that other answers had to be sought out."[6] "I told Dennis that 'limits' was not the proper word to use; that 'alternatives to growth' would be more useable. And that's the issue that I thought had to be discussed.... We should discuss things that could be accepted and alternatives that do not shut everything down."[7] As a result of their discussions, Meadows suggested that Mitchell organize a prize competition to address this question: "How might a modern society be organized to provide a good life for its citizens without requiring ever-increasing population growth, energy resource use, and physical output?"[8]

George Mitchell, heartily supported by his wife, Cynthia, responded by creating a program dedicated to the study of growth problems. He asked a small group of business leaders, educators, and futurists to develop a plan. Dennis Meadows summarized the results:

> In 1974 George Mitchell ... resolved to encourage a more positive, rigorous, and comprehensive discussion of the constraints on and the alternatives to growth. Five guidelines were adopted for this effort ... to design new social options:
>
> 1. The program should not try to prove or disprove the limits-to-growth thesis, but should search for the policy implications of a societal transition from growth of population, materials use, and energy consumption to steady state.

2. Directors of the program should seek out and encourage the participation of the best minds from a large variety of cultural, disciplinary, and ideological perspectives.

3. The emphasis should be on long-term issues, those that will confront mankind over the next thirty years or so.

4. The investigation should emphasize the use of sound empirical data and rigorous analysis to provide viable images of the future.

5. The analysis must acknowledge global interdependencies … but [specifically] stimulate development of new information useful to decision makers in the industrialized West, as they decide what must be done *by them, now,* and *within their own countries.*[9]

These guidelines were to be used in two sets of activities devoted to the transition from growth to steady state, the Woodlands Conferences and an essay competition for the Mitchell Prize. Five conferences were planned, to be completed within a decade. Each conference was to be accompanied by a prize competition. The best essays would be awarded the George and Cynthia Mitchell Prize—in later years called the International George and Cynthia Mitchell Prize for Sustainable Development. The prize was the first one dedicated to sustainable development. From the beginning it was organized as an international competition, but the perspective of developing countries received greater attention only in the 1990s.

First Woodlands Conference: Limits to Growth, 1975

The first Woodlands Conference was held in October 1975. The conference title reflected Mitchell's desire to restate the original message by the Club of Rome: "Limits to Growth: The First Biennial Assessment of Alternatives to Growth," which meant, in short, "Limits, but …" Mitchell was intimately involved in preparing the conference, more so than in later events. The problem "concerned me," he said. "Therefore I took the time to try to think out what in the world was happening."[10] Dennis Meadows and John Naisbitt, then president of the Urban Research Corporation, served as conference directors.[11]

The conference, held at the just-opened Woodlands Conference Center, was an enormous success, with five hundred attendees, large press coverage, and the excitement generated at the event. Molly Ivins, coeditor of the *Texas Observer*, said in her review of what she called the "Doom Conference": "I have seen the future, and I can tell you it is polysyllabic."[12]

The conference started from the premise that limits not only existed but were already having a negative effect on the global quality of life. Most participants agreed that there were some limits to be faced. They attempted to formulate a response: (1) Transition to steady state would have positive consequences for society provided action was taken in time; (2) Limits would have serious negative consequences if they were ignored so long that they began to intrude on social development; and (3) Growth had to be redirected by better balancing of economic, social, and environmental goals.[13]

There were forty panelists and speakers, including Jay Forrester (who had designed the computer program that was used in the *Limits to Growth* study); the British economist E. F. Schumacher (author of *Small is Beautiful*); World Watch Institute president Lester Brown; Herman Kahn, founding director of the Hudson Institute; Dr. Jonas Salk, developer of the polio vaccine; *Limits to Growth* authors Donella and Dennis Meadows; and Ian McHarg, author of *Design with Nature* and planner of The Woodlands. Other prominent speakers at the 1975 conference included Sico Mansholt (European Common Market), Amory Lovins (United Nations Environment Program), Elise Boulding (University of Colorado), U.S. senator Jacob Javits, Herman E. Daly (Louisiana State University), and Hazel Henderson (Princeton University). Many of the conference speakers became prominent in the field of sustainability studies in the years that followed.

Reminiscing, George Mitchell described the highlight of the conference: a heated debate between Dennis Meadows and Herman Kahn. Kahn, a former staff member of the RAND Corporation and founder of the Hudson Institute on future studies, spoke on the topic "Growth Is Good for You." He disagreed vehemently with the limits-to-growth thesis. Mitchell summarized Kahn's position: "Just develop everything and technology will take care of everything."[14] In Mitchell's view Meadows had the better arguments in the debate that followed Kahn's presentation, but he faced a formidable debater. Meadows put it this way: "Kahn's viewpoint, which is shared by many other people, is that there are no limits. If something like a limit starts to show up, the market and technology will finesse it and let you keep going."[15]

At the time of the 1975 Woodlands Conference, sustainability was not a household word, although the term "sustainable state" appears in one of the conference papers, "Equity, the Free Market, and the Sustainable State" by Donella Meadows.[16] She argued that the market system was inherently inequitable and unstable and should be regulated by rules that limit population and capital growth. Such "a steady-state society would automatically make the attainment of equity easier."[17] This was a position close to that of Herman Daly, who at the same conference presented a model for a steady-state economy. Such an economy, in his words, required "sharing, population control, and stabilization of average per capita resource consumption."[18] Daly later served as chief economist at the World Bank and was influential in introducing sustainability into the World Bank philosophy.

The George and Cynthia Mitchell Prize was awarded for the first time at the 1975 Woodlands Conference. Eleven hundred essay abstracts from thirty-one countries were received and judged on scholarly merits by a panel of experts. A sum of twenty thousand dollars was divided among five prize winners. The winners were Robert Allen (Switzerland), Bruce Hannon (Urbana, Illinois), Joan Davis and Samuel Mauch (Switzerland), and John Tanton (Petoski, Missouri).[19] Their essays discussed the nature of equilibrium societies, strategies for societal development, the role of energy use in economic growth, and the role of migration in world stability. The papers were printed in the conference proceedings *Alternatives to Growth*.

Second Woodlands Conference: Nature of Sustainable Societies, 1977

The 1977 conference broke new ground. The conference theme was "The Nature of Growth in Equitable and Sustainable Societies." The event attracted more than five hundred people. The Club of Rome cosponsored the meeting, and both of its leaders, King and Peccei, attended, as did the authors of the first two reports to the Club of Rome. The conference was to serve four goals:

- To bring about a better understanding ... of new and alternative approaches to growth;
- To search ... for resolution of problems induced by the disparity of material growth between developed and developing countries in the world;

- To analyze possible patterns of development which were consistent with the variety of social, institutional, and ethical systems found in the world; and

- To explore the *nature of a sustainable society* and whether it might be equitable internationally (my italics).[20]

Roundtables and workshops at the conference were all structured around the concept of a sustainable society. Among the session titles were: "Is it possible for a nation to achieve a sustainable society?" "Is there a basis of international solidarity for a just and sustainable world community?" "Social structures in a sustainable state." "Labor supply and demand in a sustainable society." "Energy alternatives." "Information systems and decision-making processes for the transition to a sustainable society." "Meeting human needs in a sustainable society." "Modern corporations in a sustainable society." "Sustainable agricultural practices." "What environmental standards should exist in the transition to a sustainable society?"

This formidable agenda was far ahead of its time. Unfortunately, no satisfactory record exists of the conference proceedings. There are only two documents I could find—the conference program (from which I took the session titles in the preceding paragraph) and a typewritten volume containing the five winning papers of the 1977 Mitchell Prize competition. The papers presented at the conference and the subsequent discussions are lost. Thus, what may have been the single most important Woodlands Conference is poorly documented. Our interviews, conducted thirty years later, yielded at least a clue to answer this question: When did the term "sustainable society" first emerge and how did it grow to dominate the 1977 conference?

Apparently the term was coined at the 1975 Woodlands Conference. Herman Daly, then professor of economics at Louisiana State University, presented a paper on "Institutions for a Steady State Economy." Such an economy, according to Daly, was "characterized by a constant population and a constant stock of physical artifacts."[21] Dennis Meadows, in his account of the 1975 Woodlands Conference, praised Daly's work as "one of the few important contributions ... to negotiate a transition from growth to steady state."[22] According to Cabell Brand, who attended the 1975 conference, Don Lesh coined the term during the discussion period that followed Daly's presentation. He argued that a sustainable society would balance material growth with environmental protection. Lesh was intimately familiar with the *Limits to Growth* debate. He was a close friend of Aurelio Peccei and served as American liaison to the Club of Rome. In 1982 he became director of the Global Tomorrow Coalition, an environmental group headquartered in Washington, D.C.

In the following year Meadows followed up on Lesh's idea and defined ten characteristics of a sustainable society (see box).[23] Using these attributes Meadows helped prepare the 1977 Woodlands Conference and suggested the conference theme: "The Nature of Growth in Equitable and Sustainable Societies."

Mitchell remembers it this way: "We coined the expression 'sustainability.'"[24] George Mitchell had now found the theme he liked. "After about two or three conferences I began to realize what we're really seeking was the *nature of sustainable societies.*" "How do we develop a technique for sustainable societies to exist?" "How could you establish sustainable societies when you have a rapid population growth?"[25]

Mitchell made these statements several years after the conferences. As time went by, Mitchell may have assigned himself a more direct role than is borne out by the memory of others: "When I started the growth issue conferences, *Limits to Growth* was our first topic. The next one concerned *Alternatives to Growth....* I knew our focus was not quite right.... Alternatives to growth didn't make sense because some growth is important, some growth is not. Finally I came up with what I think truly describes the right direction: the *Nature of Sustainable Societies.*"[26] Mitchell states: "I had never heard of it [sustainability] before. But after I started using it, I saw it begin to be used in other places."[27] Mitchell is probably mistaken when he claims to have coined the term. Even so, it is he who created the right setting for the first dialogue about sustainable societies. And he is right in describing his work over the next several decades as his search for the nature of sustainable societies.

Also in 1977, Dennis Pirages, a political science professor at the University

Characteristics of the Sustainable Society

Reestablish man's link with natural systems

Learn from living within limits

Substitute humanistic for materialistic goals

Accept limits in rich countries

Meet the needs of small communities

Focus on long-term goals

Use technology that can fail safely

Assign economic value to conservation and equity

Accept a long, slow process of revision

Rely on value changes by individuals

—Dennis Meadows, 1977

of Maryland, edited a collection of essays entitled *The Sustainable Society.*[28] The book was inspired by *The Limits to* Growth but came to the opposite conclusion: Without growth it would be difficult to improve the condition of the poor. To do so by taking from the rich was politically difficult, and only continued growth could produce and sustain an equitable society.[29] This was entirely different from the meaning given to the term "sustainable society" at the 1977 Woodlands Conference.

Close to four hundred papers were submitted for the Mitchell Prize competition that was held in conjunction with the conference. The guidelines invited authors to search for the policy implications of a societal transition from growth of population, use of materials, and energy consumption to a condition of sustainable societies. Papers would not attempt to prove or disprove the limits-to-growth thesis. They should emphasize issues that would confront humankind over the next three to four decades. They would be based on empirical data. Finally, papers should address the information needs of decision makers in industrialized countries.

The selection process proceeded in stages. Six screening institutions from around the world first evaluated the papers. International panels then identified twenty finalists and selected five prize-winning papers, each receiving a ten-thousand-dollar award.

A paper from the Netherlands evaluated the inclusion of long-range societal concerns in high-school curricula. A paper from the United Kingdom

---

Sustainable Societies

"Sustainable societies are those that are capable of reaching and then sustaining a decent quality of life for their citizens. To achieve sustainability in the world there must be a balance between things like environmental degradation, deforestation, desertification, and food availability and other resources for the amount of people we have."
—George P. Mitchell, *The Woodlands Forum* 10, no. 2 (Winter 1993–94): 3

Sustainable societies make "social and economic progress consistent with the world's finite resource base." They are "not necessarily dependent on continued growth in energy use, population, material consumption, and industrial output."
—Gerald O. Barney, director of the 1982 Woodlands Conference

Sustainable societies seek and maintain a careful balance between economic and ecological well-being. Economic well-being provides for the necessities of human life (jobs, food, shelter, sanitation, and energy). Ecological well-being sustains the natural systems on which all life depends.
—From the introduction to this book

developed a plan for the use of an oil fund from Britain's North Sea oil profits to finance the transition to a sustainable society. The third paper presented a model for an industrial corporation that included social elements in its accounting system. The remaining two papers dealt with solar energy as a sustainable technology, as opposed to the dangers associated with fossil fuels and nuclear energy.[30]

There was disagreement at the conference. A group of demonstrators came to The Woodlands to make their point outside the conference building. They were pro-growth and wanted to know "why we are trying to stop growth," remembers Mitchell. "It didn't bother us. We went right ahead and had a good conference."[31]

The conference and prize papers went beyond discussion of the steady state economy, which had dominated the 1975 conference. Two characteristics of sustainable societies were identified in 1977. First, such a society would link economic growth to social factors, such as equity within and between countries. Mitchell, perhaps more than most conference attendees, was convinced that sustainability needed to be defined differently for rich and poor countries. Second, government and business in a sustainable society would promote environmentally friendly technologies.

The first two conferences had made a significant contribution by bringing the Club of Rome findings to the United States. Allen Commander, a faculty member of the University of Houston who helped organize the 1977 conference, summarized the impact: "The [first two conferences] got the problems surfaced and discussed at the highest levels of government. The issues were brought to the attention of public policy makers and private sector decision makers. In addition, they educated the public about the magnitude of the problems, their complexities, and that the United States could take a leadership role in solving these problems."[32]

Third Woodlands Conference: Management of Sustainable Growth, 1979

The 1979 conference was cosponsored by the University of Houston and the Aspen Institute. At one of the earlier Aspen Institute meetings Mitchell had met Harlan Cleveland, who was at the time director of the institute's international affairs program. Previously he had held high positions in Washington and had served as an adviser to Presidents Kennedy and Johnson. Cleveland was interested in growth issues, particularly at the international level.[33] Mitchell now asked him to take the lead in preparing the 1979 conference. Cleveland got help from James Coomer, dean of social sciences at the University of Houston–Clear Lake, and from John and Magda McHale, two prominent futurists.[34] The McHales felt that limits to growth as an issue had been discussed to death and that the 1979 conference should leave that behind and instead discuss the management of sustainable growth.

Cleveland's worldwide connections helped in organizing preliminary consultations in Europe, Japan, and Mexico. Advance workshops dealt with bioresources, work and education, information and communications, the economics of the future and the future of economics, and a summer session on "The Limits to Government."

Mitchell, as he had done for the previous conferences, provided the bulk of the conference funding, which by now had risen to $250,000. In addition, he underwrote $90,000 for the nine Mitchell Prizes that were awarded that year. For the first time the winners were ranked. Paul Ehrlich, a population specialist from Stanford University, received the first prize for his paper on "Diversity and the Steady State." He argued that biological diversity was important for maintaining or restoring a desirable future state.

Cleveland also commissioned ten papers, which were used as benchmarks around which the substance of the conference was structured. The addition of commissioned papers to the open prize competition reflected disappointment with the quality and vision of the prize papers that had been received in previous years. Dennis Meadows told it bluntly: "I was ... surprised and disappointed at the relatively trivial, simplistic, and ... ineffective ideas that we generated with the prize.... I didn't consider that the prize process was generating value commensurate with the amount of money that George was putting into it."[35]

Two volumes of proceedings were published. One, *The Management of Sustainable Growth*, edited by Harland Cleveland, contained the commissioned papers. The other volume, *Quest for a Sustainable Society*, edited by James C. Coomer, included the nine Mitchell Prize essays.[36]

Cleveland's retrospective on the conference reveals the dramatic difference in thinking about growth problems that had occurred since the 1975 Woodlands Conference: "The Meadows team had complicated computer projections of how we were going to run out of oil, iron, copper, and other resources in a certain year. But there were two things wrong with that. First, it turned out we weren't going to run out anywhere as soon as they thought. And, second, they had overlooked two major resources in our economy—invention and knowledge."[37]

By 1979 the fear of too much growth that had driven the limits-to-growth debate was gone. New information showed that the population explosion would be contained by 2050. There would be rapid population growth for another two generations, but then the population increase would slow and eventually stabilize. New sectors of the economy were emerging, in particular electronics and information services, as well as biotechnology. Alexander King, Harland Cleveland, and the McHales had just organized an international conference where scholars had presented evidence about the large potential for developing renewable resources.[38] Once renewable bioresources were added to calculations, some nonrenewable resources would last longer than previously estimated. The newly emerging industries were less energy intensive and required smaller inputs of materials. The nature of economic growth was changing. The United States and other industrial societies were already in transition toward a new stage of growth that was neither unrestricted material growth nor no-growth. The conference discussed this more sustainable form of growth and the changes it required in management and governance.[39]

Willard Wirtz, a former U.S. secretary of labor, captured the changed intellectual climate that permeated discussions at the conference: "'Growth' includes whatever contributes to the common opportunity to make the highest and best use of the human experience." Cleveland was convinced that the world would not run out of resources, because it had expanded its ways of thinking about resources.[40] Maurice Strong, the architect of the 1972 Stockholm Conference on the Environment, stated that sustainability was needed at the global level to improve living conditions in the third world. He proposed different development strategies for rich and poor countries. A shift to qualitative growth—he called it "new growth"—was needed in industrialized countries. In addition, they had to make a massive commitment to the development of the developing countries, where traditional means for stimulating growth had to be used.[41]

One trend disturbed Mitchell: the conferences attracted mostly academics and few businessmen. Also, in 1979 there was again controversy at the conference. The story is told by Robert Chianese, who was one of the year's Mitchell Prize winners. He writes how he had enjoyed the meeting and the variety of viewpoints presented by true believers in the cause of sustainability: "There was Paul Ehrlich ... the first place prize winner of the year, who warned about vanishing biodiversity. David Hopcraft, a rancher from Kenya, explained the practicality and profitability of sustainable meat production by replacing imported livestock with indigenous game animals. In addition, James Garbarino, a sociologist, applied sustainable strategies to policies involving children." But then the prizewinners had to listen to House Speaker Tip O'Neill, House majority leader Jim Wright, and Senator Lloyd Bentsen, who spoke at the awards gala dinner and advocated opposite ideas—on the need to increase spending for weapons and the need for more offshore drilling of oil. Chianese comments: "We wondered if we were being asked to support those very destructive growth policies which our prize-winning papers had argued against. As a result, a few of us ... held a press conference to protest the speakers and their treatment of sustainability. While our actions made headlines in the Houston newspapers, they left a sour taste in my mouth."[42]

There was another remarkable event. David Gottlieb, a long-time associate of George Mitchell, tells the story of how the then-famous Ehrlich-Simon wager originated at the 1979 conference. This, in his view, was the highlight of the conference.[43] The wager received much national attention, including an article in the *New York Times*.

> Julian Simon challenged environmental scientists to bet against him on
> trends in prices of commodities, asserting that humanity would never
> run out of anything. Paul [Ehrlich] and the other scientists knew that the
> five metals in the proposed wager were not critical indicators and said
> so at the time. They emphasized that the depletion of so-called renew-
> able resources—environmental resources such as soils, forests, species
> diversity, and groundwater—is much more indicative of the deteriorating
> state of society's life-support systems.... Nonetheless, after consulting
> with many colleagues, Paul and Berkeley physicists John Harte and John
> Holdren accepted Simon's challenge in late 1980.[44]

Julian Simon won the wager because the price of three of the five metals went down in absolute terms and all five of the metals fell in price in inflation-adjusted values. So, per the terms of the wager, Ehrlich paid Simon the difference in price between the same quantity of metals in 1980 and 1990 (which was $576.07).[45] In 1990 Ehrlich and Steven Schneider, a climatologist at Stanford, offered a new wager, this time focused on the declining buffering capacity of the earth for human activities. But Simon declined.

Fourth Woodlands Conference: Role of the Private Sector, 1982

Sometime in the early eighties, the cooperation with the Club of Rome and Dennis Meadows ended. There was no break but a sense that the focus of the Woodlands Conference series was moving away from the *Limits to Growth* agenda. Meadows's original plan had been to publish five volumes on the Alternatives to Growth theme, one for each conference in the ten-year cycle. He completed only the first one. The 1977 proceedings never materialized, and the 1979 proceedings had a different focus.

The 1982 Woodlands Conference and Mitchell Prize competition explored an aspect of sustainability that did not interest Meadows but was central to Mitchell's agenda—*The Future and the Private Sector*.[46] Mitchell retained Gerald O. Barney to serve as conference director. This shows how Mitchell operated in preparing for the conferences: "I usually picked people between conferences, outstanding people that did work around the world on sustainability issues."[47] Barney had just served as study director of the Carter administration's *Global 2000* report (see chapter 6). "Barney had done this work for the [Carter] administration and therefore was familiar with the things we were trying to put together."[48]

"The conference focused on how a productive and profitable private sector could contribute to sustainable societies both worldwide and in the specific context of the Mexico–United States region."[49] Barney divided the conference in two parts. The first highlighted constructive contributions by the private sector to the resolution of world problems and was titled "The Roles of the Private Sector in Achievement and Maintenance of Sustainable Societies." The second part focused on global problems as perceived by the private sector. The program agenda also included an update on the Reagan administration's progress in following up on the *Global 2000* results and a discussion of the recently issued Brandt report on North-South relations. The conference rapporteur summarized the consensus of the meeting: "The need to alter many trends in human affairs and to develop strategies for a *transition to a sustainable society* is evident from economic disruptions: growing needs for energy, food and water; expanding deserts; atmospheric modifications;... and continued population growth."[50]

While this was an important conclusion, the conference turned out to be less successful than the previous ones—the agenda covered too much ground and attendance was down, in particular the private sector was poorly represented, even though the conference was intended for that audience. This was the biggest disappointment for Mitchell: "We had an enormous interest in the academic world and the environmental world but a very poor attendance, in all conferences, from the private sector. We really wanted desperately to get them interested."[51] He was also concerned about the rapidly rising cost— $725,000 was spent on the 1982 conference.[52]

The Mitchell Prize was for the first time funded at the level of one hundred thousand dollars. The first-place winner received thirty thousand dollars, the second-place winner twenty thousand dollars, and the remainder was divided among nine competitors. Orville Freeman, a former U.S. secretary of agriculture, and Ruth Karen received the first prize for their paper "The Farmer and the Money Economy: Role of the Private Sector in Agricultural Development of LDCs." Judging criteria for the essay competition emphasized originality, practicality, and utility—a more down-to-earth approach than in previous competitions. More than three hundred abstracts of proposed essays on roles of the private sector in the transition to sustainable societies were received.

Transition to Houston Advanced Research Center (HARC)

Following the original plan, a fifth Woodlands Conference and Mitchell Prize competition was to be held in 1984 to round out the ten-year program that had been announced in 1974. This did not happen. There were several reasons for George Mitchell to pause and rethink his strategy.

He was satisfied that something significant had been accomplished. No other group—private or public—had devoted similar energy and resources to a multiyear effort to understand the changing nature of economic growth and the characteristics of sustainable societies.

At the same time, there was room for improvement. Interest in the themes of limits to growth, alternatives to growth, and the nature of sustainable societies had waned. Attendance at the conferences had declined. There was little evidence that the conferences had made a lasting impact.[53] A meeting of the board of directors overseeing the Woodlands Conferences, held shortly after the 1982 conference, concluded that the program had lost steam. Attendance at that conference had reached 339 persons only by giving scholarships to half of the attendees. The directors added: "The program was not focused for taking action, but was generally good for new information."[54]

The Mitchell Prize papers were informative and innovative. Yet they did not add up to a grand new strategy for the future. Taken together they had not met Mitchell's hope that the world's best minds would define a roadmap toward sustainability. Dennis Meadows, who had first suggested the prize competition to Mitchell, now concluded: "When I first helped you develop the plans for the Mitchell Prize, I assumed there was a great deal of relevant wisdom, which only had to be brought together. I was wrong. There are many wise people concerned about the issues [related to building sustainable societies], but they do not know the answers."[55] David Gottlieb, who had helped with the early conferences from his position as dean of the College of Social Sciences at the University of Houston, confirmed this view: "There was the hope that some of these papers would get international attention and lead to policy changes. I never really saw how that would happen."[56]

The strain of preparing major biannual conferences and prize competitions had grown. Conference directors changed from one event to the next. Mitchell had chosen directors who had a national reputation. But they lived far away and did little to ensure continuity and follow up. Mitchell had assigned the heavy logistical task of conference management to the public relations department of his energy company. Its staff measured the success or failure of each event by the extent of media attention, which had been high in the beginning but declined to almost zero in 1982. Joe Kutchin, who had headed the MND Public Relations Department since 1974, felt that little had been accomplished: "When you look back ... and say that with all the effort and all the expenditure and all the high-powered intellect that we got together, what came out of it? Very little."[57] This may be true of many conferences if one ignores the value of providing opportunities for exchange of information, debate, and networking. But this is difficult to document. And if these outcomes had occurred at the Woodlands conferences, it had been mostly of benefit to academics, not to business executives and policy makers that Mitchell most cared about. In the future more might be achieved if local conference directors were hired who, in addition to being knowledgeable about sustainability issues, would bring continuity to Mitchell's sustainability program.

Another reason for a temporary pause was that Mitchell himself had developed new interests that competed, at least for a while, with his commitment to sustainability. By the 1980s the Texas economy was shedding its dependence on oil and gas. The state now sought new economic vigor from companies specializing in high technology. Mitchell eagerly followed these developments and wanted to make sure that the Houston region, and especially The Woodlands, benefited from new economic opportunities. He considered these trends in reorganizing his sustainability program. It took several years and another of Mitchell's ventures into new territory before the two interests came together.

In 1974, when Mitchell had started the Woodlands Conferences series, he had created the Woodlands Center for Growth Studies. The center's first task was to organize the Woodlands Conferences and Mitchell Prize competitions. Yet Mitchell wanted the center to serve a larger agenda:

> To educate the public by means of organizing and directing conferences, seminars and meetings, and by publishing articles, books, and general periodical literature and by use of mass media to bring public attention to certain global issues. These issues include, but are not necessarily limited to, population growth, use of resources, quality of environment, economic conditions and urbanization.[58]

For the first ten years, the center remained an empty shell without staff or resources to develop such an ambitious program. Beginning in the mid-eighties conditions slowly changed and allowed the center to work more deliberately on the 1974 mission statement. The trigger for change was the creation of the Houston Advanced Research Center—HARC.

HARC was another Mitchell venture. He founded HARC in 1982 as a nonprofit research organization to conduct cooperative research by four Texas universities—Texas A&M, Houston, Rice, and Texas at Austin. HARC was to manage joint projects that were too large or too ambitious for a single university. The focus was on technological innovation—superconducting magnets, lasers, seismic imaging, image compression, supercomputing, and similar technological breakthroughs with a potential for economic applications. The research consortium got off to a splendid start when it received government funding to develop the magnets for the Superconducting Super Collider that was then being built near Dallas. Much progress was made in developing a more efficient magnet design. Several years into the project, however, the federal government selected a more conventional, though less sophisticated magnet design. Then Congress killed the entire project, leaving the field to the European Organization for Nuclear Research (CERN) in Geneva, Switzerland. From that point forward HARC was forced to work on smaller projects. It held on for twenty years but never generated enough income to support all of its research centers.

HARC had been designed with the model of North Carolina's Research Triangle Park in mind. Mitchell visited the North Carolina institutes and commissioned Arthur D. Little to assess the prospects for creating a similar research facility in The Woodlands. Their study concluded that HARC could become the anchor for bringing science and technology companies to The Woodlands—a strategy that turned out to be moderately successful. Today, The Woodlands is home to forty thousand jobs, including many in science and engineering. But no large high-technology firm has moved to The Woodlands. To this day the scale of research and development activities remains far below that of Research Triangle Park.

At first, Mitchell saw no connection between HARC and his work on sustainability. "But then as we got into doing things at HARC, we wanted HARC to do more about sustainability," he recalled.[59] In 1985 W. Arthur "Skip" Porter became the first president of HARC. Porter enthusiastically supported the idea to reactivate the Center for Growth Studies and make it a part of HARC. "It seemed to me that HARC was in a position between the Woodlands Conference events to have the intellectual energy to maintain ongoing dialog that would connect one conference to the next."[60] After discussions with Porter, Mitchell drafted a new mission statement for the Center for Growth Studies that was even broader than the 1974 version. He outlined an ambitious program:

How well humankind manages earth's resources, environment, and population will determine whether civilization advances or dies in coming years. These three issues are worldwide in importance and scope.... Mismanagement of the earth's resources, environment, and population policies manifests itself, among other ways, in deforestation, desertification, water shortages, famine, climatic changes, poverty, and political and social instability....

The Center is to undertake programs which advance the [following] concepts:

First, *foresight capability*, at least at the national level, is essential ... so that the best possible near-term and long-term projections can be made.

Second, *economic development*—particularly in the Third World—is a handmaiden to programs that would successfully deal with issues of resources, population, and environment.

Third, the *business community*, both U.S. and international, has great contributions to make, and efforts should be expended to enlist its intellectual and financial participation.

Fourth, the ultimate goal is a *sustainable society*, which ... is one that husbands resources wisely, respects the environment, practices enlightened population policies, and promotes development, all in order that opportunity for good nourishment, protection against the elements and disease, and opportunity for economic and social improvement are available everywhere.[61] (my italics).

From 1985 to 2001 this broad mandate guided the work of the Center for Growth Studies—later called the Mitchell Center—as it operated as the smallest of HARC's research centers.

CHAPTER 6

Washington Takes Note

Global 2000 Report to the President

In his 1977 message on the environment, President Jimmy Carter instructed Thomas Pickering at the State Department and Gus Speth at the Council on Environmental Quality to prepare a wide-ranging study to serve as the foundation for long-term environmental policy planning.

The resulting massive study, *The Global 2000 Report to the President: Entering the Twenty-first Century*, dealt with the growth, scarcity, and ecological problems the world was likely to encounter by the year 2000 if present policies continued. The range of problems examined was broader than in *The Limits to Growth*. For example, water scarcity and climate change were included. While the emphasis was on the need for improved facts, studies, models, and review mechanisms, there was some discussion of needed action: "The available evidence leaves no doubt that the world—including this Nation—faces enormous, urgent, and complex problems in the decades immediately ahead. Prompt and vigorous changes in public policy around the world are needed to avoid or minimize these problems before they become unmanageable. Long lead times are required for effective action. If decisions are delayed until the problems become worse, options for effective action will be severely reduced."[1]

Study director Gerald O. Barney, a physicist by training (and director of the 1982 Woodlands Conference), drew upon the informational resources of thirteen federal agencies, including the departments of State, Agriculture, Energy, and the Interior and the Central Intelligence Agency. He found the various government agencies woefully unprepared for dealing with the new problems created by growth and resource constraints.[2] Agencies used models with different assumptions and methods to project trends in their areas of responsibility. Modeling across agency boundaries did not exist. The report stated: "The executive agencies of the U.S. government are not now capable of presenting the President with internally consistent projections of world trends in population, resources, and the environment for the next two decades."[3]

Presidential Directive for the Global 2000 Report

"I am directing the Council on Environmental Quality and the Department of State … to make a … study of the probable changes in the world's population, natural resources, and the environment through the end of the century. This study will serve as the foundation of our longer-term planning."
—President Jimmy Carter, May 23, 1977

The report opens with a prediction for the year 2000: "If present trends continue, the world in 2000 will be more crowded, more polluted, less stable ecologically, and more vulnerable to disruption than the world we live in now. Serious stress, involving population, resources, and environment are clearly visible ahead. Despite greater material output, the world's people will be poorer in many ways than they are today."[4]

The report concludes that "the problems of preserving the carrying capacity of the earth and sustaining the possibility of a decent life for the human beings that inhabit it are enormous and close upon us."[5]

The Global 2000 Report sold 1 million copies in six languages. Herman Kahn and Julian Simon published a stunning critique of the report, very much in the tradition of the Kahn critique of *The Limits to Growth*. They wrote: "We are confident that the nature of the physical world permits continued improvement in humankind's economic lot in the long run, indefinitely. Of course there are always newly arising local problems, shortages and pollutions, due to climate or to increased population and income. Sometimes temporary large-scale problems arise. But the nature of the world's physical conditions and the resilience in a well-functioning economic and social system enable us to overcome such problems, and the solutions usually leave us better off than if the problem had never arisen; that is the great lesson to be learned from human history."[6] The chasm between the positions of "caution: trouble is looming ahead" and "go on: growth is good for you" had not narrowed since the 1975 Woodlands Conference confrontation between Kahn and Meadows.

The report did not find a warm reception at other agencies of the Carter administration. In particular the Office of Management and Budget and the president's science adviser criticized many technical details and felt that better data could have been used.[7]

The Global 2000 Report to the President Entering the Twenty-First Century Volume One

Figure 9. Cover of *The Global 2000 Report to the President*, 1980.

Yet George Mitchell liked the report and took it as a starting point for his efforts to make Washington more responsive to the idea of sustainability. Cabell Brand told me that Mitchell "bought 1,000 copies of [the book] and distributed it to the whole business roundtable, to all YPO members, and the CEO of every company that he could think of. He hoped that it would lead to increased federal attention to global issues."[8] Mitchell began a campaign to institutionalize monitoring of and reporting on global issues as a continuing effort of the federal government. In his words the federal government needed to "develop foresight capability." To make his case, Mitchell frequently traveled to Washington and met with elected and executive officials. His main point was that *The Global 2000 Report* was a good beginning. But a single report was not enough. Information had to be updated regularly and brought to the attention of policy makers and a large public audience. The government must begin by "getting the facts together."[9] On different occasions he met with former President Carter, Senators Timothy Wirth and Al Gore, and Gus Speth, who had overseen preparation of the report. Mitchell also testified before congressional committees. At one hearing he was part of a group of business leaders, among them Ted Turner, discussing the need for government action in support of sustainability.

Mitchell did not succeed in his campaign to educate and motivate federal policy makers. He recalls: "It's been very difficult to get the Congress to understand sustainability.... We have got to get the politicians to think that way. They don't think that way. We have got a few but not many."[10] After trying for years, Mitchell gave up hope that the government would develop an early warning system—foresight capability—to address the increasing number of unsustainable conditions. Instead, he turned to the National Academy of Sciences (see chapter 8).

The Global Possible

After publication of *The Global 2000 Report*, scholars and the media increasingly used the words "global issues" instead of "growth issues," which had dominated the debate in the 1970s. The new term gradually shifted the debate from concern about resource scarcity to the even more ominous signs of human-caused changes to natural systems, including acidification of soils and lakes, depletion of the ozone layer, and global climate change—issues that would come to the forefront during the 1980s and 1990s.

Yet the attention the Carter administration had given to global issues did not last long. While environmental protection had figured among the priorities of previous Republican administrations—President Nixon had created the Environmental Protection Agency and had appointed William Ruckelshaus as its first administrator—this was no longer the case under President Ronald Reagan. He and his conservative cabinet followed the thinking of Kahn and Simon: The market and technology will take care of problems. In Europe sustainability concerns narrowed to acid rain and forest decline. In Germany these reached a fever pitch during the 1980s. In the United States, absent government action, nongovernmental organizations took the lead in analyzing threats to sustainability and identifying possible remedies.

Gus Speth had used his position at the Council on Environmental Quality and his role in overseeing *The Global 2000 Report* to coordinate the work of federal agencies on global issues. He had now left the government. With support from the MacArthur Foundation he founded the World Resources Institute (WRI) in Washington, D.C., and soon demonstrated the power of a nongovernmental organization in educating the nation and the world about global issues. Mitchell served on WRI's board of directors for many years though he did not attend as many meetings as Speth would have liked.[11]

In 1984 WRI convened an important conference called "The Global Possible: Resources, Development and the New Century." A stellar cast from industry, science, and government attended, among them George Mitchell. Perhaps the single most important outcome was an action agenda that focused on "things to do here and now," rather than on the endless debate about a far-distant sustainable future. The conference identified detailed, immediate steps that would get the country going on the road to a sustainable world. Specifically, actions were proposed to advance five transitions:

- A demographic transition to a stable world population;
- An energy transition to an era in which energy is produced and used at high efficiency without aggravating resource scarcity and atmospheric pollution;

Figure 10. Cover of *The Global Possible*, 1985.

- A resource transition to reliance on nature's "income" and not depletion of its "capital";
- An economic transition to sustainable growth and a broader sharing of its benefits; and
- A political transition to a global bargain grounded in complementary objectives between North and South.[12]

The report described how timely action in each of these areas would create a "brighter and sustainable future." What would be accomplished?

World population is stabilized before it doubles again, and the erosion of the planet's renewable resource base—the forests, fisheries, agricultural lands, wildlife, and biological diversity is halted. Societies pursue management practices that stress reliance on the "income" from these renewable resources, not a depletion of the planet's "capital." . . . People and resources are protected from the costly consequences of pollution and toxification and from disruptive climate change. . . . Manufacturing processes produce less waste, and what waste is produced is reused in other processes. Advanced technologies are widely applied to achieve high efficiencies in the use of energy. . . . Broadly based economic growth proceeds in ways that lessen the gap between rich and poor both within and among countries, and the door is increasingly opened to artistic and cultural pursuits in a world where the hard labor of survival is lessened.[13]

The volume of conference papers covered the entire range of the new agenda: population, poverty, third-world cities, water, forests, biological diversity, energy, atmosphere, minerals, and oceans. The volume's definition of sustainability foreshadowed the 1987 United Nations report: "At the core of the ideal of sustainability . . . is the concept that current decisions should not damage prospects for maintaining or improving living standards in the future."[14]

CHAPTER 7

The Mitchell Center, 1984–2001

The Center for Growth Studies, which Mitchell had created in 1974 when he planned the Woodlands Conferences, became operational only after he created the Houston Advanced Research Center (HARC) in 1982. He had given the center its name assuming that the "limits to growth" and "alternatives to growth" debates would dominate the search for sustainability. Yet by the mid 1980s, the name no longer resonated with the sustainability movement. People thought that the center was busying itself with real estate or local development issues. Economic and population growth and scarcity of natural resources were no longer viewed as the main problems facing humankind. Instead, most countries eagerly clamored for more growth, and the debate had shifted from pollution and resource scarcity to impairment of nature's global systems. Considering these trends, a new name was chosen in 1988—Center for Global Studies.

This choice was partly driven by the desire to keep the same initials, CGS. But the new name also reflected growing scientific evidence that the pace and scale of development now had the power to interfere with the functioning of life-supporting natural systems—air, water, and land. People had used them as free sinks to absorb waste and pollution, only gradually realizing that this was a costly mistake. The new threats to sustainability included climate change, acid deposition, destruction of the ozone shield, loss of biodiversity, increased soil salinity, desertification, water scarcity, destruction of rainforests, and the growth of megacities. All of these conditions were the result of human actions. The issues were complex and often not fully understood. They impacted economic growth; they caused serious, perhaps irreversible, damage; and solutions or coping strategies needed to be developed amidst continuing uncertainty and controversy.

In 2001 the center's name was changed again, to the Mitchell Center for

Sustainable Development. I will use the name Mitchell Center in the follow-ing discussion covering the years 1984 to 2001.

During the 1980s and the 1990s, the Mitchell Center grew gradually. In 1986 I took a half-time position as center director, which I held for fifteen years. I started alone; eventually we had a professional team of six and an annual budget just shy of 1 million dollars. We kept busy organizing confer-ences and the Mitchell Prize competition, but we also conducted research and outreach programs. In addition to my work at the Mitchell Center I taught natural resources policy at the University of Texas. I made the two jobs com-patible by organizing student research projects in support of research we were doing at HARC. Each year I lead a two-semester policy research project with ten to fifteen graduate students who worked on some aspect of sustainability. One year we would do background research for an upcoming Mitchell Center activity; in other years we would take on specific tasks as part of an ongoing center project. Over the years we trained almost two hundred students to do research on sustainability.

Mitchell continued to provide financial support for the ongoing Wood-lands Conferences and the Mitchell Prize, and for the publication of the *Woodlands Forum*, the brainchild of the Communications Department of Mitchell Energy and Development Corporation. The *Forum* was a biannual journal on sustainability that we distributed at no cost to a large mailing list from 1984 to 1994. In addition to news items, each issue featured one or sev-eral in-depth interviews with national and international leaders engaged in sustainable development research or policy. In all, the editors conducted more than one hundred interviews with individuals active in the field of sustainable development. Many of the leaders of the nascent sustainability movement were featured: Lester Brown, Gro Harlem Brundtland, Jimmy Carter, Chris-topher Flavin, Tim Mahoney, Dennis Meadows, Michael Oppenheimer, Rus-sell Peterson, William Ruckelshaus, Rafael Salas, Gus Speth, Maurice Strong, Russell Train, Ted Turner, and Timothy Wirth. Given Mitchell's interest in involving the business community, other interviews were conducted with presidents of leading companies who had an interest in sustainability: Applied Energy Services, Atlantic Richfield, AT&T, BP America, Control Data Corpo-ration, DuPont, Enron, IBM, MCC, Monsanto, Union Carbide, Unocal, USX, and Weyerhaeuser.

Following the broad mandate given to the center, we also carried out research and outreach projects that were funded from grants by private foundations and the federal government. Over the years the center succeeded in getting grants from major foundations—Ford, Hewlett, Turner, the Houston Endowment, Brown, Meadows—and public agencies—the National Science Foundation, Environmental Protection Agency, National Oceanic and Atmospheric Administration, and the World Bank. In most projects the center's staff served as project planners, team managers, and research assistants; in addition, we hired university faculty and graduate students to participate as expert consultants or research assistants. Our projects were all interdisciplinary, with natural and social scientists working as a team.

Mitchell was not involved in the day-to-day operation of the center. But he followed closely what we did. I met with him regularly, and we made frequent reports to HARC's board of directors of which he was a member. Without him we would not have had the resources and the support of HARC's president and board that we needed. When we got started, research centers on sustainability were still rare. Lester Brown had founded the Worldwatch Institute in 1974. The Rocky Mountain Institute and the World Resources Institute were set up in 1982, also by leaders in the sustainability field, Armory Lovins and Gus Speth.

Defining a Research Niche

The Mitchell mandate for the center was broad, which presented a challenge. Given the center's small size, it was important to work on a carefully selected subset of the global issues agenda, and we decided to focus our research, outreach, and conferences on the regional impacts of global sustainability issues.

Mitchell supported the decision to focus on local and regional issues. But it must be said that his heart was always at the global and national levels, where he was most eager to make a contribution. There were times when he and I disagreed on the center's ability to contribute to the resolution of global issues. But over time Mitchell agreed that global issues had important regional dimensions that needed to be studied. At times we also differed on priorities. For Mitchell the Woodlands Conferences remained the heart of the center's program. For me, conferences were of interest to the extent they were linked to ongoing or planned research. We found ways to combine these two visions. The Woodlands Conference on climate change led to major research projects in Brazil and on the border with Mexico. Another Woodlands Conference highlighted the center's contribution to the work of the National Academy of Sciences, where Mitchell was supporting the Global Commons project (see chapter 8).

The center's regional focus was driven by this question: How did the newly emerging global issues play out in places with different economic, social, and environmental characteristics? Using the example of climate change, carbon dioxide and methane emitted anywhere in the world contribute to the buildup of greenhouse gases. This is a global phenomenon that causes changes in temperature and precipitation, rise in sea level, and, possibly, extreme weather events. But the exact changes in temperature, rainfall, sea level, and extreme weather will be different from place to place, depending on geography and level of development. It is this connection between global causes and place-based impacts that was at the heart of our work.

We did our fieldwork in three places: the Rio Grande basin on the border with Mexico, Northeast Brazil, and the Houston metropolitan area. Houston was an obvious choice, given our location within the Houston metroplex. Northeast Brazil and the Rio Grande faced similar problems: a semiarid climate, scarce water resources, growing population, and a high incidence of poverty. In both regions, water availability and population growth have been on a collision course. We wanted to understand how the new global issues further complicate this situation and what regional response strategies might be formulated. Our research focused on these themes: (1) assessing the impact of climate change on water resources, (2) developing a methodology for conducting sustainability assessments, and (3) linking experts to citizens in sustainability planning.

Fifth Woodlands Conference: The Regions and Global Warming, 1991

Using the regional approach as an entry point, the Mitchell Center in 1991 organized the fifth Woodlands Conference, "The Regions and Global Warming: Impacts and Response Strategies." By this time there was a fast-growing literature on the causes of global warming and ways to reduce greenhouse gas emissions. But less attention had been devoted to regional impacts of and adaptive responses to the likely climate of the future. The conference was designed to review what was known, to identify knowledge gaps, and to plan new research programs. There was great interest in the topic, as evidenced by the conference sponsors: United Nations Environment Program, World Meteorological Organization, U.S. Environmental Protection Agency, and Oak Ridge National Laboratory.

Speakers at the conference summarized current knowledge about the regional and local dimensions of climate change and about policy options that were appropriate for different regions of the world. Special attention was given to developing countries, which faced added risks caused by poverty and population growth. Working groups at the conference examined impacts on and response strategies for agriculture, forestry, coastal areas, and semiarid regions. We asked participants in the conference to draft and debate a summary statement of findings and recommendations, a practice borrowed from the American Assembly at Columbia University, which has a long tradition of convening conferences with a focus on current policy.

The American Assembly, founded by President Dwight Eisenhower when he was at the helm of Columbia University, engages conference attendees as active participants, not just listeners. Participants are sent study materials in advance to read at home or during the flight to the conference. Only a few overview papers are presented at the outset of the conference. This frees up time for participants to work in small teams on particular aspects of the conference theme. Each group, at the end of three half-day sessions, drafts a short statement of findings and policy recommendations. Two or three editors use these statements to prepare, in a grueling night-long effort, a draft conference report. All participants spend the last morning of the conference debating and amending this statement. The final version is printed within days after the conference and distributed to a wide audience. The method is work intensive but succeeds in actively engaging conference attendees and quickly disseminating the conference's accomplishments.

The report developed at the 1991 conference stated that enough information existed to include climate change in regional planning. Until then, planners had pointed to the uncertainty about regional impacts and had not considered climate change in conjunction with other development problems faced by the region. The time had come to change this practice. "Regionally based strategies can take advantage of the community of interests that exist as

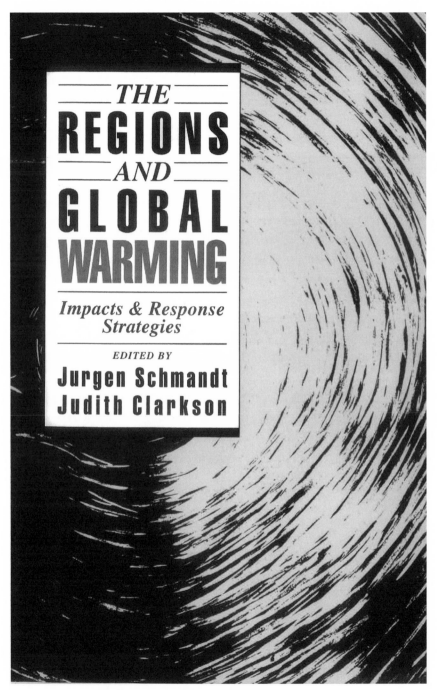

Figure 11. Cover of *The Regions and Global Warming*, 1992.

the result of common geography, likely consequences of climate change, interconnected economies or similar history.... Perhaps the simplest approach is to utilize modern or historical correlations between regional temperature, precipitation variations, and vegetation growth to predict the effects of future climate change on agricultural production and natural vegetation.... Global warming responses should be linked to existing programs for energy conservation, soil and water conservation, sustainable agriculture, and sustainable urban development."

The Mitchell Prize was again awarded at the level of one hundred thousand dollars. A hard-working international panel of judges, including a Dutch Nobel Prize winner, a Russian academician, and the president of an Indian nonprofit organization ranked the papers received and selected eight prizewinners. Three of them came from developing countries. The first prize went to Daniel Botkin, a well-known biologist, and the second prize to José Goldenberg, Brazil's minister of education at the time. Oxford University Press published the Mitchell Prize papers as well as a selection of other papers presented at the conference.[1]

Botkin's prizewinning paper used the regional impacts of climate change on the Great Lakes to raise fundamental questions about sustainability.[2] He argued that progress toward sustainability was slow because policy makers and resource managers have a flawed understanding of sustainability. They strive for a static sustainable state that is both "good" for all life and "desirable" for people. Such a state does not exist. In reality, ecological systems are nonlinear and constantly changing. In his words: "The correct approach to management of our natural resources at a regional level requires two fundamental changes: a change in our deepest beliefs about nature and, as a consequence, a development of realistic quantitative methods to allow us to make projections of likely effects of our activities.... Thus, as we move away from the old ideas, we will need to recast the concept of sustainability."[3]

An important innovation was added to the prize competition: Ten young scientists received a Young Scholars Award for an outstanding research proposal on a specific aspect of sustainable development. A year later the winners were invited back to The Woodlands to report on the results of their projects. Over the years this practice led to successful interactions between senior and junior prizewinners and lively seminars with the young scholars.

The conference laid the foundation for the Mitchell Center's followup work in the Rio Grande basin and Brazil. Conference participants helped draw up initial plans for these projects. Both were aimed at identifying regional sustainability problems and developing action strategies to deal with them.

Sustainability Assessment

The Colorado and the Rio Grande are the main rivers in the American West. In both rivers water is shared with Mexico (see Figure 12). The Rio Grande (called the Río Bravo in Mexico) originates east of the Rocky Mountains in the Colorado mountains. From El Paso to the Gulf of Mexico the river forms the international border between Mexico and the United States. Irrigated agriculture has long been the economic backbone of the region, both in Texas and in northern Mexico. Most of the Upper Rio Grande waters have been used up by the time the river reaches Fort Quitman, an hour's drive below El Paso. Therefore, the Lower Rio Grande Valley—the most populous part of the basin—depends on water from two tributaries, the Pecos in the United States and the Conchos in Mexico. Two international reservoirs, Amistad and Falcon, store water from these tributaries. For agriculture and cities in the Lower Rio Grande Valley, these reservoirs are the sole source of water because groundwater in the region is naturally saline.

The center's previous work on climate change and water resources in Texas had shown that water supply in the Lower Rio Grande was highly sensitive to climate change. In the new study we asked how climate change would impact existing concerns, such as periodic droughts and floods, competition for water between agriculture and cities, deteriorating water quality, reduction of instream flow and loss of biodiversity.

The central question was this: Will there be enough water, of acceptable quality, to support sustainable development in the Rio Grande Valley to the year 2030? The assessment was conducted by a binational team of specialists in hydrology, water quality, ecology, demographics, economic development, and water management.

There were several important findings.[4] First, irrigated agriculture uses 88 percent of available river water. Improvements in water distribution and use, water metering, and changes in crop patterns can maintain current crop yields while reducing water use by 40 percent. Second, urban and industrial

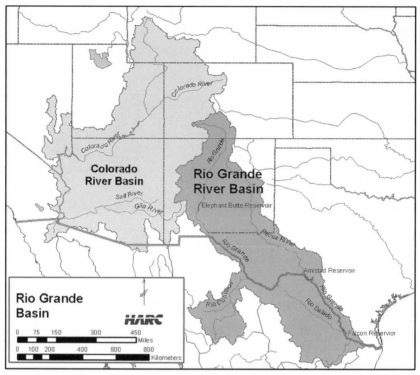

Figure 12. The Colorado and Rio Grande basins. (Source: Houston Advanced Research Center)

activities use 12 percent of river water. To meet the demands of the projected population growth by 2030, the share of municipal and industrial water use must rise to 20 percent. Third, a substantial amount of agricultural water will need to be transferred to the cities. To do this by law will be controversial because it would affect the existing rights of water users. A better solution would be to develop a regional water market modeled on California's successful water market, which has helped the state to cope with drought.[5] But while Texas law allows for the selling of water rights, Mexican law does not and would have to be changed. A fourth finding was that the region has already suffered significant damage to aquatic and terrestrial resources. While full restoration is unlikely, governments can still act to prevent further deterioration. Fifth, desalinization of brackish groundwater or seawater is not yet cost effective but will be in the near future. Sixth, a multiyear drought would require exceptionally large transfers of water from irrigation to municipal use. Agricultural production would be severely constrained.

Sustainability Planning

Sustainable development requires more than *substantive* changes in policy. Equally important are changes in *how* policy is planned, implemented, and enforced. For sharing common resources, a communal or grassroots approach may work better than top-down control by large administrative agencies. This is the case, in particular, when the former free sharing of the resource must be controlled to prevent overuse—the medieval commons problem discussed in the introduction. Elinor Ostrom has identified conditions under which shareholders are willing to serve the common interest by yielding some of their previous rights.[6] Boundaries of the shared property are clearly defined, rules fit local conditions, stakeholders participate in rule making, guardians are locally appointed, sanctions are graduated, and conflicts are resolved quickly.[7] Mitch Mathis, a Mitchell Young Scholar and subsequent staff member at the Mitchell Center, researched a hundred-year-old water-sharing program in a drought-prone area of Northeast Brazil. He found that farmers relied on trust and networking in designing and maintaining a shared water system among themselves.[8]

Northeast Brazil

The Mitchell Center used Ostrom's theoretical framework and Mathis's familiarity with Brazil in cooperative work with Brazilian scholars in a large World Bank project in Northeast Brazil. The project had real impact in improving living conditions in the region, where underdevelopment persisted despite a sustained public policy effort. The results of over twenty years of intensive World Bank support for the region were meager, mostly due to an overemphasis on technical studies and a failure to create social capacity for change. The new project, called ARIDAS, was to address this shortcoming. The project team of some twenty experts examined economic, political, social, and environmental factors that influence development. The topics studied included drought, climate variability, soil erosion, inadequate farming techniques, unequal land tenure, lack of water resources (especially for nonlandowners), education, sanitation, health, and lack of infrastructure for irrigation and industrial development. Citizen groups then used this information to develop policy recommendations. The written output, resulting from the dialogue between citizens and experts, amounted to fifty volumes.[9]

The ARIDAS strategy aimed at visualizing a new future for the region. Three questions were asked of both citizens and experts: What is sustainable or unsustainable in the Northeast today? If we continue along current paths, how sustainable or unsustainable will the future be? What kind of a future do we desire?

To help answer these questions the researchers developed a business-as-usual scenario (years 2000, 2010, and 2020) based on population projections and continuation of current economic and social trends; developed a desired sustainable development scenario for the future, based on broad input from members of the civil society in the states of the Northeast; analyzed future vulnerability to climate variability, in particular droughts; prepared a sustainable development strategy; and drafted sustainable development plans for each state and each economic sector. Detailed citizen input was obtained by means of a survey and workshops. Participants included representatives of business, church, agriculture, unions, local government, and nongovernmental organizations. Many people took part that had never before been consulted on issues of public policy.

In the survey, participants were asked what is unacceptable in the present and what the desired future would look like. Respondents were encouraged to be specific and to rank priorities in terms of importance, feasibility, barriers, and resource intensity. The following issues emerged as the critical issues facing the future of the Northeast: education; organization and participation of civil society; political will; modification of the agrarian structure; training of the workforce; technology; societal oversight of government; extension of irrigation; medical services; the environment; and birth control.

Toward the end of the project, citizen workshops were held in all nine states of the Northeast region. Each involved participants from church groups, nongovernmental organizations, labor unions, and community associations. Government officials were not asked to attend so that an action agenda could be developed solely by local stakeholders. (Governmental and elected officials would later play an important role at the regional workshop and final conference.)

The policy recommendations developed by the ARIDAS team had considerable impact. In particular, Ceára, one of the poorest states in the Northeast, systematically reformed education, health services, rural development, and water management using the sustainable development perspective and policy recommendations of the ARIDAS reports. The Mitchell Center helped state authorities to improve methods for relocating farmers who lost their land to new reservoirs.[10] The reform effort continues to this day. The project also caused change at the grassroots. Many nongovernmental organizations in the region became familiar with the principles of sustainable development and began to apply them in their work. The project was well received at the World Bank, which used project results in subsequent project funding in Brazil.

Houston Environmental Foresight
The Foresight Program, supported by the Houston Endowment and the Environmental Protection Agency, was conducted by the Mitchell Center to establish environmental priorities for the eight-county Houston region. The project was part of a national EPA program aimed at assisting communities to develop risk-based environmental strategies. Our project went beyond the initial EPA initiative by organizing a consensus process after technical studies had been completed.[11] David Hitchcock, John Wilson, and Sabrina Strawn were the Mitchell Center staff members responsible for this project.

We began by convening a community forum, called the Foresight Committee, for the constructive discussion of environmental concerns. Members came from the eight counties in the Houston region. They represented the interests of business, environmental protection, rural areas, the inner city, and government. About one-third represented major ethnic groups in the Houston region: African American, Asian American, and Latino. The committee held regular meetings during a two-year period from 1994 to 1996.

We received help from about one hundred volunteer scientists and other experts whose work was coordinated by a small Foresight Science Panel. The experts used existing sources to compile the best available scientific evidence covering twenty areas of environmental concerns in the region. The results were published in a volume called *Houston Environment*.[12]

The Foresight Committee then used a consensus process to rank the severity of problems identified by the experts, narrowing the list to outdoor air pollution, indoor contamination, habitat alteration and loss, and the scarcity of parks as the most troublesome environmental problems in the region. Of these, controlling air pollution, outdoors as well as indoors, was seen as the highest priority for the region.[13] This served as the starting point for Houston mayor Lee Brown's subsequent Air Summit and as a major impetus for his air-quality initiative.

During a second phase of the project (1997–2000) working groups of more than 140 regional stakeholders representing environmental, government, business, and citizens' groups assembled to discuss issues ranked as "highest" and "high" priority and to recommend strategies to address them. They issued reports on outdoor and indoor air quality; habitat, parks, and water issues; toxins and contaminants; and water quality.[14] As a final step, the Mitchell Center convened a symposium, "State of the Region's Environment."

Houston Environmental Foresight led to the creation of the Gulf Coast Institute, which provides a forum for addressing growth and sustainability issues in the region. Mitchell Center staff also played a major role in drafting the award-winning *Houston Corridor Guide to Sustainable Development*, published by the City of Houston's Planning and Development Department, which the U.S. Department of Housing and Urban Development has since used in its training programs.

Civic Science

Out of the work on these three case studies—the Rio Grande, Northeast Brazil, and Houston Environmental Foresight—the center developed a methodology for the conduct of sustainability assessments. First, experts from different scientific disciplines analyze information to identify problems and their likely development over time. Second, citizens are convened to express constituent values and goals. Pursued in parallel, not sequentially, this is the main characteristic of what we call *civic science*—the structured interaction between scientific experts and citizen representatives. Such an interactive process offers "citizens" and "experts" opportunities for organized, recurrent dialogue. The dialogue serves not only as a means for sharing scarce resources (informational, technical, human, and financial) but also as a critical procedural step in the synthesis of positions and ideas as well as the preparation of policy recommendations.[15]

Sustainability planning is most likely to succeed when input by experts and stakeholders proceeds on parallel and interactive tracks.

While each track has its own identity and produces its own record of activity, the two maintain ongoing communication with each other through regular meetings where representatives evaluate progress, exchange relevant information, and discuss next steps. The ultimate goal of those working within each track is similar, such as improving quality of life, adapting to climate change, alleviating poverty, or managing drought. Yet the immediate interests, methods, and language of each will differ significantly from the other. Experts seek verifiable data. Citizens seek mutually acceptable reforms. These differences must be mediated by skillful track leaders lest they lead to misunderstandings or a sense that the other's work is irrelevant or inapplicable to the problem at hand.

The civic science model offers a new way for linking expert knowledge to decision making. The model is work intensive and time consuming but well suited for reaching consensus on shared natural resources and environmental concerns.

CHAPTER 8

National Academy of Sciences

President Carter's *Global 2000 Report* had convinced George Mitchell that the federal government needed a long-term program to summarize new research findings on global issues and present the results in nontechnical reports to policy makers. Such a program would be an important step on the road to sustainability. Over time, leadership and action would follow. Mitchell felt that the country was not yet ready for the massive changes in policy that were needed to implement sustainability. In the interim, the country needed to develop, as he liked to call it, "foresight capability." This became the focus of Mitchell's efforts to advance sustainability at the national level: "I am sure that it is best to concentrate on a limited number of global issues; that encouraging Congress to develop foresight capabilities is a high priority.... My main objective ... is to achieve enactment of government foresight legislation at the federal level."[1] He followed with interest congressional initiatives in this area. Senator Al Gore had introduced a bill to create an Office of Critical Trend Analysis. When this led nowhere, Mitchell put his hopes on the promotion of environmental stewardship championed by Senator Tim Wirth from Colorado.[2] Again, these efforts faltered.

After years of lobbying for federal action, Mitchell concluded that the U.S. government was not ready to engage in even precautionary study and planning in order to face emerging global issues. So he began to look for alternatives. He searched for the best institution in the country to regularly update *The Global 2000 Report* and, on a continuing basis, generate reliable information on sustainability. He liked the work of nongovernmental organizations such as the World Resources Institute and the Worldwatch Institute. But he was afraid that they did not carry enough weight and could easily be ignored by policy makers. Eventually, he concluded that the National Academy of Sciences "had the best ability" to advise the government on emerging issues. The Academy, in his view, did high-quality work that was nonpartisan and respected by both Democratic and Republican administrations. His vision for working with the Academy, then and to this day, was long term: "I'm trying to get information and data on all the major issues facing us, like population, resource depletion, deforestation and others.... If all worked as planned, we would have a major report on growth topics issued every four years with each cycle of government. And every year we would have a highlight, like global warming one year or air pollution another. But every four years we would be brought up to date with the available knowledge about these population problems."[3]

What drew Mitchell to the National Academy of Sciences was its prestigious tradition of advising the government on scientific and technical matters. The Academy serves two functions. First, senior scientists elect new members who meet and present scientific papers to each other. This is the traditional honorary role of scientific societies the world over. Second, the Academy also functions as a scientific advisor to the federal government. Since 1863, and reconfirmed in 1916, Congress gave it this duty: "[T]he Academy shall, whenever called upon by any department of the Government, investigate, examine, experiment, and report upon any subject of science or art."[4]

In this advisory capacity the Academy operates through the National Research Council. The council has grown into a vast operation with an expert staff of over a thousand and an elaborate committee structure covering most fields of science, engineering, and medicine. Ad hoc committees are established to work on specific projects. Committee members are selected nationwide, and occasionally internationally. Most of them are not members of the Academy but are known for their expertise on the issue at hand. They serve without compensation and are reimbursed only for travel expenses. Either at the request of Congress or the executive branch, or, rarely, on its own initiative, the Academy will review existing research on a current policy issue. In each case the Academy goes through an elaborate procedure: convene a committee of experts, provide the committee with professional staff assistance, research the issue, carefully review the committee's report, and then present research findings and policy recommendations to the government and the public. Reports are published by an in-house publishing house, the National Academy Press.

The Academy serves both its honorary and advisory functions in three branches: the National Academy of Sciences, the National Academy of

Engineering, and the Institute of Medicine. The three institutions together
are often referred to as the National Academies.[5]

Mitchell "discovered" the Academy through his long-time friend Cabell
Brand, a businessman and former State Department staffer. Brand knew
Washington, and also President Carter, Gus Speth, and Frank Press. Press
had left a prestigious career at MIT to serve as Carter's science adviser. He then
served as president of the National Academy of Sciences from 1981 to 1993. In
the mid-eighties Cabell introduced Mitchell to Press, who organized a small
meeting with Al Gore, then a congressman, to discuss Mitchell's interest in
foresight. Brand recalls: "After the meeting, George and I talked with Frank
Press. And we said, Frank, you've got to get the business community involved.
As a result of George's insistence, Frank Press started the President's Circle."[6]
This group was first convened in 1989. Initially it had about thirty members,
among them many business leaders. Brand, Mitchell, and Bill Miller, who had
served as Carter's secretary of the treasury, were charter members. The group
met several times a year for informal discussions. Mitchell talked to the group
about his interest in sustainability and foresight capability. Several private
meetings between Mitchell, Brand, and Press followed.[7]

William Colglazier, the executive officer of the National Academy of
Sciences, recalled that Mitchell "had always been pressing the Academies
to take a bigger role related to sustainability issues or as he called [it] the
Global Commons. And the Academy, on our side, was trying to figure out
what would be our unique niche, how we could really contribute to this very
broad vision that George had laid out."[8] Mitchell himself put it this way: "So
I thought if we could work with [the Academy] to get some action, it would
be helpful. I proposed to Frank Press that I would support a study of the National Academy on sustainability."[9] Out of the discussions with Press and his
staff came a proposal, refined over the course of several years, to organize the
"Global Commons Project"—a multiyear research program designed to better understand the linkages between economic development and humanity's
global commons of atmosphere, land, and water. The program would also be
a venue for bringing the results of Academy studies to the attention of the private sector. This reflected Mitchell's conviction that business would become a
strong actor in promoting sustainability.

The Global Commons Project was finally launched in 1994. Mitchell
provided a grant of 1 million dollars, and the Academy, in a highly unusual

move, added 2 million dollars of its own funds.[10] The Academy convened a twenty-four-member Board on Sustainable Development. The board spent almost an entire year educating itself on sustainability.[11] Then, instead of following the Global Commons outline, it set out to answer this question: How can the research community help policy makers and business leaders in meeting the basic requirements for feeding, housing, educating, and employing 3 billion more people by 2050? Board members felt that answering this question was an appropriate task for a research institution. The Academy would identify the scientific underpinnings of needed policy measures and thereby supplement the work of policy advisory bodies in the field of sustainable development. Two such bodies had been convened at about the same time, the President's Council on Sustainable Development and the World Business Council for Sustainable Development.[12]

The Board on Sustainable Development made a second decision on how to frame its work: Members agreed that sustainability could only be achieved as the result of an evolutionary learning process. They defined the next fifty years as the transition period to sustainability and focused their study on this time frame. The transition period would be a period of trial and error, searching for the right answers. At the end of the fifty years, 95 percent of the demographic transition to a more stable world population would have occurred. By that time a more sustainable balance between economic and environmental priorities had to be in place. Bruce Alberts, who in 1993 had taken over the presidency of the National Academy of Sciences, "saw in the idea of a sustainability transition the great challenge of the coming century" and committed the Academy "to explore and articulate how the science and technology enterprise could provide the knowledge and know-how to help enable that transition."[13] The results of the Global Commons Project were published in a 1999 report, *Our Common Journey: A Transition toward Sustainability.* The report was widely circulated—Mitchell sent the book to a thousand business leaders—and was in its third printing at the time of this writing.

Our Common Journey

The report starts with the observation that scientists have made great progress in understanding and managing single-issue environmental threats, such as air and water pollution, acid rain, or depletion of the ozone layer. However, they have much to learn in understanding the causes, pathways, and impacts of *problem clusters* that have arisen in recent times and are caused by multiple, cumulative, and interactive stresses from human activities. Sustainable development is needed to solve these problems; sustainability science is needed to understand them. *Our Common Journey* identifies the methods, institutions, and funding requirements of sustainability science. The term aptly summarizes the work described in the report, but it was only coined toward the end of the drafting period. Robert Kates, one of the report's principal authors, recalls that Bruce Alberts, after reading the draft, first spoke of sustainability science.[14]

In the case of traditional environmental threats, where a specific disturbance of a natural system by human action needs to be understood, scientists have successfully used the traditional tools of science—formulating a hypothesis, observation, measurements, interpretation, and linking data to theory—to explain the issue and provide policy makers with a knowledge base that can guide remedial action.

However, single-issue problems, in the view of the Academy report, are no longer the key obstacles standing in the way of sustainable development. Instead humanity is now facing environmental threats that arise from multiple, cumulative, and interactive stresses driven by a variety of human activities. Two examples: many regions suffer from the combined stresses of population growth, water pollution, and ill health; other areas experience the joint effects of soil depletion, drought, and malnutrition. Problem clusters of this kind are difficult to unravel and complex to manage. They also tend to be shaped by physical, ecological, and social interactions in particular places. The importance of the last point was particularly stressed by Pamela Matson, a sustainable development board member who had done extensive fieldwork with farmers in Mexico: "I think I was the one person on the board, at that moment, who was actively engaged in a place where different stresses were interacting, and affecting the decisions that people were making and the consequences for their environment. And I just knew that the same things were not playing out in the same combinations everywhere else."[15]

The report suggests that sustainability science can unravel such complex problem clusters to their constituent components, follow their interactions, present an *integrated* view of the issue, and identify options for workable solutions. The report concludes: "Developing an integrated and place-based

Figure 13. Cover of *Our Common Journey*, 1999.

understanding of such threats and the options for dealing with them is a central challenge for ... a transition toward sustainability." Ralph Cicerone, who was a member of the Board on Sustainable Development and became president of the National Academy of Sciences in 2006, offered this definition: "Sustainability science is supposed to draw upon contributions from every field of science and engineering and medicine, social science, and draw upon the observations of the direction we're headed and the likely outcomes and continue to navigate this transition to a more sustainable direction."[16]

This is not a revolution in scientific theory or method. Rather, sustainability science requires scientists to organize their work differently. Scientists committed to sustainability science will work in teams whose members are trained in different disciplines. They will use the methods they have been trained in to study parts of the problem cluster. They will then work as a group to integrate their findings. They also will take the time to interact closely and repeatedly with stakeholders and decision makers. Finally, they will present their results in a format that is accessible to the nonspecialist.

Cicerone believed that "the concepts [of sustainability science] are turning out to be long lasting, and they're very durable and very robust."[17] He added a revealing comparison: Europe is ahead in political awareness of issues threatening the global commons, but the United States is more advanced in using an appropriate scientific framework to understand the issues and identify policy solutions that can work. But much remains to be done on strengthening the science-policy connection. William Clark, one of the authors of *Our Common Journey*, argued for a stronger involvement of scientists in the policy process: "The research community needs to complement its historic role in identifying problems of sustainability with a greater willingness to join with the development and other communities to work on practical solutions to those problems."[18]

Pamela Matson brought back what she had learned to her campus. The experience, in her words, changed the school of earth sciences which she led, and all of Stanford University: "The goals as laid out in *Our Common Journey*—meeting the needs of people, sustaining the life support systems of the planet—[taught us] that this isn't about just the environment. We have worked very hard to harness the strengths that we have throughout the university ... around sustainability. I feel incredibly lucky to have been part of that whole thing. It changed my life."[19] She added that students "voted with their feet" by streaming to the problem-solving, interdisciplinary approach that Stanford was introducing.

Mitchell was impressed by the Academy report. "*Our Common Journey*, defining the road toward sustainability, is a landmark of what should be done on trying to get sustainable."[20] He liked that the Academy actively shared the study results with science academies from other countries. Influential meetings were held in New Delhi and Tokyo. He also was pleased to see that the Academy leadership consulted with their counterparts in the academies of engineering and medicine to promote a sustainability perspective throughout the academy complex. Mitchell's positive reaction was not shared by some of his business friends. Cabell Brand, for example, would have preferred that a more action- and business-oriented strategy result from the Mitchell grant.

The true significance of the Academy approach is made clearer by an example from the past. In the first half of the nineteenth century cholera struck ferociously in the growing urban centers of Europe and America. It took many years for British physicians to discover that contaminated drinking water caused cholera. Once the cause was known, remedial action was taken swiftly, primarily by building urban sanitation and drinking water systems. The disease was successfully controlled because of new scientific knowledge. A more recent example is the discovery by scientists that newly developed chemicals with great economic utility—chlorofluorocarbons used widely for cooling between the 1950s and 1980s—also damaged the ozone layer and thereby reduced the earth's protection from excessive solar radiation. Without this scientific finding it would have been impossible to know how to prevent increasing damage to plants and humans. Sustainability science provides the essential link between global environmental threats and successful countermeasures. It draws a roadmap that governments, business, and civic organizations can use in policy development. Mitchell understood this: Without scientists first unraveling the complexity of global issues political, solutions will fall short of providing solid answers.

Sixth Woodlands Conference: Managing the Transition, 1997

In 1997, halfway through the Academy's work on *Our Common Journey*, the Mitchell Center, jointly with the De Lang Endowment at Rice University, organized the sixth Woodlands Conference. The conference title was "Sustainable Development: Managing the Transition." Five hundred individuals attended. They came from a variety of fields, including science, religion, business, administration, and politics, to discuss, debate, and provide insight into the concept of "transition to sustainable development," which was central to the Academy approach. The conference papers, *Sustainable Development: The Challenge of Transition*, were published by Cambridge University Press.[21]

The conference had two goals. First, the Academy presented preliminary findings of its Mitchell-sponsored study to the public. The Academy speakers focused on the concept of a transition to sustainability: the next fifty years during which world population would increase by another 3 billion people. From then on the population pressure would ease. The transition challenge was awesome: How can humankind provide food, energy, jobs, services, and a decent standard of living for an additional 3 billion people without irreversible damage to air, water, and land? Bruce Alberts, president of the National Academy of Sciences, defined the contribution of science to meeting the challenge:

> An overall vision for ... a transition to sustainability in the twenty-first century ... would require that the world provide the energy, materials, and knowledge to feed, house, nurture, educate, and employ many more people than are alive today—while preserving the basic life support systems of the planet and reducing hunger and poverty. Such a profound and unprecedented transition has no charted course. Science can help provide direction by identifying the energy, materials, and knowledge requirements for the transition; the crucial indicators of unsustainability; the levers of change to move us towards sustainability; and the measurements needed to report on our progress.[22]

Robert W. Kates, who together with William Clark had directed the team that wrote *Our Common Journey*, argued in his keynote address that a successful transition period to sustainable development must limit growth of population as well as consumption. Between now and 2050, population growth will be contained. But more people will live on earth than ever before. Acceptable living conditions can only be sustained by reducing consumption. "Learning to manage consumption at a level equivalent to population may be the major challenge of a sustainability transition," he said.[23] History shows that growth

Sustainable Development

The Challenge of Transition

Edited by Jurgen Schmandt *and* C H Ward

Figure 14. Cover of *Sustainable Development: The Challenge of Transition*, 2000.

rates of food, energy, and the economy exceed population growth by factors of 2, 4, and 8, respectively. This is not sustainable into the future. "Global capitalism seems inherently based on growth ... of both the number of consumers and their consumption.... A sustainability transition might require profound changes in the making and selling of things—shrinking energy and material throughputs, substituting information for energy and materials, creating a standard for satiation [and] sublimating the possession of things for that of the global commons."[24] Kates spoke in 1997. His conclusion is similar to that of *The Limits to Growth*, published twenty-five years earlier.

The conference then engaged in its second task: sketching a *road map* for the journey toward sustainability during the next fifty years. The conference statement, prepared by several working groups and debated intensely during the concluding half-day plenary session, emphasized many factors that the Academy work did not address, including value changes, voluntary measures, and, above all, the creation of a shared vision of a sustainable and desirable society: "With a common language on sustainability we can develop a broad understanding so that individual action is part of a synergistic and comprehensive approach to sustainability that leverages all sectors of society" (see Appendix 4 for the text of the conference report).

For the first time the International Mitchell Prize was awarded to a single individual rather than to several recipients. Instead of an essay competition, as in the past, a committee appointed by the National Academy of Sciences solicited nominations and submitted their recommendation to George Mitchell. The 1997 winner of the one-hundred-thousand-dollar prize was Marcelo C. de Andrade from Brazil who was honored for "his efforts to encourage the active commitment and involvement of corporations in the conservation and sustainable development of tropical resources and the communities that depend on them."[25] Andrade had founded Pro-Natura International, a nonprofit organization, first in Brazil and then in other parts of the world. Pro-Natura facilitates cooperation between local stakeholders and developers in forest management and preservation of ecosystems.

Seventh Woodlands Conference: Corporate Capabilities and Tools, 2001

As part of the Global Commons Project of the National Academy of Sciences, George Mitchell obtained funds from the Turner Foundation to study how business corporations can thrive and at the same time apply principles of sustainability.

The Mitchell Center convened a series of workshops and conducted case studies. They showed that sustainable development, rather than limiting corporate growth, offered real opportunities for business in meeting human needs in the twenty-first century. The 2001 Woodlands Conference, "Corporate Capabilities and Tools: Making Sustainability Work in the Twenty-first Century," presented the results of this work. Preparation of the case studies and organization of the conference was the work of Mitchell Center staff member Marilu Hastings.

The case studies were of five large corporations that identified a wide range of strategies to drive their businesses to pursue sustainability.[26] *Alcoa*, the world's largest producer of aluminum and alumina, participates in all major segments of the industry: mining, refining, smelting, fabricating, and recycling. The issue of global climate change is particularly important for the aluminum industry because of its energy-intensive nature and the relationship between energy from coal, oil and gas, and greenhouse gas emissions. Alcoa has taking steps to both reduce these emissions and support impartial analysis of the global climate change issue. The company is heavily involved in various aspects of industrial ecology, from reducing waste to process redesign. The company also has implemented policies that require environmental impact studies to be completed before new bauxite mines are established overseas. An internal audit system evaluates each of the company's business units according to three criteria: economic, environmental, and safety. Each carries equal weight.

Enron, at the height of its short lifespan, was the largest wholesaler of electricity, the top producer of solar cells and wind turbines, the biggest marketer of natural gas, and one of the leading gas exploration and transmission companies in the United States. Despite its reliance on fossil fuels as its major product, Enron actively participated in the global climate change debate. Its efforts in developing alternative energy sources were an indication that the firm was well aware of the potential market opportunities available through the transformation of the energy sector. The firm invested aggressively in developing renewable energy sources and the infrastructure to use them, especially wind and solar. Enron emphasized the environmental advantages of natural gas, compared to coals and oil, as a bridge fuel toward long-term sustainable energy supplies.

Ford Motor Company developed a strong focus on clean cars. The company has embarked on several initiatives to integrate environmental priorities into its vehicle lines, operations, and corporate culture. In 1997 Ford's board of directors formed a committee to review company strategies on environmental and public policy issues, including global climate change, fuel economy, alternative fuels and electric vehicles, vehicle recyclability, and the environmental impacts of the company's facilities. The company dominates the alternative-fueled vehicle market in the United States. It has taken a lead in using recycled material in its cars, as well as recycling the cars themselves. Its research agenda includes alternative fuels, emission reduction, and fuel efficiency. Ford is adopting and implementing the ISO 14001 environmental management standards at its facilities worldwide. The company's goal is to achieve continuous environmental improvement at its facilities.

Formosa Plastics Corporation is the largest polyvinyl chloride maker in the world. Its Texas (FPC-TX) facility responded to concerns about environmental impacts and compliance by working with local residents and stakeholders to negotiate an agreement that satisfies the company and the community. As a result, FPC-USA signed an agreement that allows extensive stakeholder involvement in the operation of the Texas facility. A second agreement addresses concerns about wastewater discharges. In 1997 local representatives and company officials signed a joint sustainable development agreement. This agreement is designed to introduce sustainability into company operations.

The *Royal Dutch/Shell Group* of companies learned valuable lessons from its failure to attend to environmental concerns in Nigeria and Brent Spar. After the media had drawn worldwide attention to these disasters, Shell saw its financial performance threatened unless it changed its business model. In 1996 Shell undertook a thorough review of what its stakeholders and the public expected from the company. A new "Statement of General Business Principles" reflected greater emphasis on environmental and social issues. Sustainable development concepts were integrated into the statement. The Shell Group's particular programs involve several initiatives, including balancing economic, environmental, and social goals; addressing global climate change; and integrating social capital and sustainable development features into company performance. Shell also initiated new procedures for the environmentally and socially responsible management of its oil and gas exploration sites.

At the Woodlands Conference, executives from the five case study companies discussed how and why their corporations decided to pursue sustainability. Their success stories were aimed at encouraging other private industry representatives to search for a pathway to sustainability in their own firms. Peter Senge, who had won the Mitchell Prize in 1982, presented the keynote address on corporate learning for sustainability.

Following the recommendation of the selection committee convened by the National Academy of Sciences, the Mitchell Prize was awarded to Ray Anderson for his work in using principles of sustainability to change his company, Interface, Inc. Trained as an industrial engineer at Georgia Tech, Anderson founded Interface in Atlanta in 1973 and built it into a billion-dollar-a-year enterprise, the world's largest rug company. But every year his factories released large volumes of wastewater and nearly nine hundred pollutants. After ten to fifteen years the carpets would end up in landfills, and this petroleum-derived waste product contributed to pollution of groundwater.

Paul Hawken's book *The Ecology of Commerce*[27] motivated Anderson to turn Interface into an environmentally friendly operation—a project that he hoped to complete by 2020. Anderson's own book, *Mid-Course Correction*, recounted his "awakening" and the seven steps he took to reform his company: eliminating waste, eliminating harmful emissions, using only renewable energy, adopting closed-loop processes, using resource-efficient transportation, energizing all of the company's stakeholders around the vision, and shifting his business from the sale of a product to the sale of a service, which obliges Interface to recycle its products at the end of their useful life.[28] At the time he wrote his book in 1996, Anderson had increased the company's resource efficiency by 22.5 percent in just three years. During the same period the Interface share price had tripled.[29] His credo is short and to the point: "I believe that in the twenty-first century, the most resource-efficient companies will win."[30]

CHAPTER 9

The New Houston Advanced Research Center (HARC)

At the turn of the century, the Mitchell Center at HARC was doing well. Yet the other HARC centers, which were focused on emerging technologies, had fallen on hard times financially and a major restructuring became necessary. Over the years the four founding universities—Houston, Rice, Texas A&M, and Texas at Austin—had decided that no project was so big or so complex that only a joint effort would succeed. That removed the original reason for which HARC had been created: to function as a cooperative research organization in charge of large research programs shared by Texas universities and coordinated by HARC. Once this growth path had been closed, HARC had focused on sound engineering projects but had failed to become self-sustaining. The organization had survived thanks only to subsidies from George Mitchell.

After nearly two decades of trying to make the model of a multicenter research organization work, the HARC board of directors concluded that the organization lacked a clear mission focus: was it energy, image compression, super computers, or sustainability? The directors decided that HARC should shed much of its engineering work and adopt as its single mission the promotion of sustainability at the regional level. Thus the small Mitchell Center became the nucleus of the new HARC. Todd Mitchell, son of George Mitchell, took on the task of managing the transition. Over the course of five years, he built a smaller, focused research organization that serves the Houston and Gulf Coast region, perpetuating the interest in sustainability of HARC's founder and building on the Mitchell Center's successful work in the field. Rebuilding HARC was difficult, and many believed that it could not be done. But with the right ideas, people, and determination, the research organization successfully embraced sustainability as its mission.

Predictably, a number of challenges arose during the rebuilding process. As an organization focused on technological innovation, HARC had been an easy fit with Houston's conservative political leadership. The new HARC, with its focus on sustainability, had to prove that it was not part of the environmental "fringe" but could bring valuable ideas to the community. Gaining the trust of business and government became a key goal of HARC's new programs.

Then there was the "two cultures" problem—natural versus social sciences.[1] The old HARC, except for the Mitchell Center, had been run by highly specialized engineers and natural scientists. Only a few of them would comfortably adjust their work to the new emphasis on sustainability. The new HARC relied less on invention per se and more on creating and communicating user-friendly science. This type of work does not appeal to the researcher who is primarily interested in producing and publishing new knowledge. It does appeal to the researcher who likes to work with colleagues from different fields in the natural and social sciences and with members of the user community, such as nonprofits, business, and government. Fortunately, the organizational transition progressed gradually, so that the shock of downsizing and refocusing only temporarily disturbed the remaining staff. Even so, it took four difficult years to achieve a new level of stability. HARC now employs about fifty scientists and support staff.

The smaller size helped to bring the budget under control. There were still red numbers during the first years, but the deficits got smaller. In 2005, the books were finally balanced. When this goal was in sight and the viability of the new HARC had been proven, George Mitchell created a 25-million-dollar endowment for the organization. The endowment income guarantees that HARC will be able to continue its work for many years to come. It also makes planning more predictable. The previous practice of asking Mitchell for an annual subsidy is no longer necessary.

HARC's regional focus was redefined as the Greater Houston area and the upper Texas Gulf Coast. Work on the Texas-Mexico border that had been important at the Mitchell Center was gradually phased out. This was the single most painful decision from my perspective. We had worked with Mexican colleagues for more than a decade and had been successful in collaborating with them on border issues and introducing them to the practice of sustainability science. But it made sense to strengthen the program in the region close to our home base. The option of expanding our reach remained open once programs in the Houston region and the upper Texas coast were firmly established.

The Greater Houston area encompasses ten counties with a population of 5.7 million people in 2008. Population will grow to over 8 million by 2030. Providing housing, jobs, transportation, education, and health services for this population while protecting environmental quality will be a monumental challenge. The upper Texas Gulf Coast supports onshore and offshore industries, fishing, and tourism. Its rich coastal ecosystems are situated along North America's most important migratory bird flyway. Land subsidence, ecosystem fragmentation, sea-level rise, invasion of exotic species, increased storm activity, and decreasing freshwater flows into bays and estuaries are among the challenges that will increase in magnitude as coastal communities grow and the impacts of climate change are felt. The HARC region, with a metroplex at the center of an environmentally sensitive coastal area, represents an ideal laboratory for developing and testing sustainability science, with potential broader application to other regions.

From 2002 to 2005 the entire staff spent much time and effort developing a common understanding of what it means to work as a regional research organization in the emerging field of sustainability studies. The resulting strategic plan summarized the operating philosophy of HARC under the motto "Moving knowledge to action to improve human well-being and the environment."[2] The central question was: How do we best analyze the interactions between natural and social systems in our region? To educate ourselves we read books and articles on sustainable development, including the Mitchell-sponsored study on sustainability science, *Our Common Journey*.[3] We also focused on the work of David Guston because it helped us to better define a research organization that is focused on the application of sustainability science.

Guston had done research on how to improve the connection between knowledge and its use in solving real world problems. He argued that this was best done by a "boundary organization [that] gives both the policy-makers and the scientists an opportunity to construct the boundary between their enterprises in a way favorable to their own perspectives."[4] David Cash addressed the same issue and offered a more descriptive definition: "Efforts to mobilize science and technology for sustainability are more likely to be effective when they manage boundaries between knowledge and action in ways that simultaneously enhance the salience, credibility, and legitimacy of the information they produce. Effective systems apply a variety of institutional mechanisms that facilitate communication, translation, and mediation across boundaries."[5] Civic science, sustainability science, and now boundary science all grapple with the same issues: bridging the gap between nature and society, between experts and decision makers, and between global and local scales.

We concluded that the new HARC must strive to facilitate movement of knowledge across the divide between *producers* of knowledge (in science and engineering communities) to *users* of knowledge (in policymaking and technology-adopting communities). With this mission HARC occupies a middle space in both the science-to-technology and the science-to-policy processes. In technology development, HARC plays a bridging role, helping to advance technologies through the so-called Chasm or Valley of Death where great ideas often fail due to lack of evaluation, demonstration, and precommercial innovation. In policy development, HARC works with decision makers to define problems and with the science community to fill knowledge gaps and integrate policy-relevant findings.

Robert Harriss, HARC's president since 2006, applied the concept of the boundary organization to HARC's most immediate challenge. He argued that a better linkage between sustainability research and action is most needed in America's growing megacities. To meet their needs he proposed that the federal government create "regional urban sustainability centers." Such centers "would catalyze, facilitate, and support the integration process necessary to creating use-inspired solutions to the grand challenges facing American cities—shaping the transition to a renewable energy future, adaptation to climate change, sustaining biodiversity and ecosystems services, reducing vulnerabilities to pollution and natural disasters, etc."[6]

The United States has created and supported boundary institutions in the past. For a century and a half, land-grant colleges and the agricultural extension service successfully linked knowledge to the needs of rural America. A new metropolitan research service would do the same for urban America, facilitating interactions between "producers" and "users" of scientific information in the country's large cities. This became the challenging vision for HARC, which built directly on the civic science model that the Mitchell Center had previously developed. HARC's current projects are refining the model of the boundary organization and applying the concept of civic science. This work will lay the foundation for a Houston municipal research service. It is hoped that HARC's experience will also serve as a prototype that other metropolitan areas can emulate.

HARC is now organized around three program areas: air and climate; clean energy; and land, water, and people. The air and climate program best illustrates how HARC uses the concepts of sustainability science and the boundary organization in practice.

Houston, as a result of the massive presence of refineries, has a serious air pollution problem. The city and neighboring counties have never met the one-hour federal standard for ozone concentrations. The current eight-hour standard allows for averaging concentrations over a longer time period. While this has moved Houston from "serious" to "moderate" noncompliance, it does not reduce the economic risk of EPA penalties and the very real risks to human health. The problem in Houston has grown over many years. Mitigation strategies were hard to design because precise knowledge about the sources, amounts, timing, and transport of pollutant releases was either missing or difficult to access by regulators. Dallas has a different industrial base but faces a similar problem.

To generate policy-relevant information, HARC worked with the Greater Houston Partnership to establish the Texas Environmental Research Consortium (TERC).[7] TERC began in 2002 and developed a nationally recognized research and policy information program. It is directed by a board of local policy

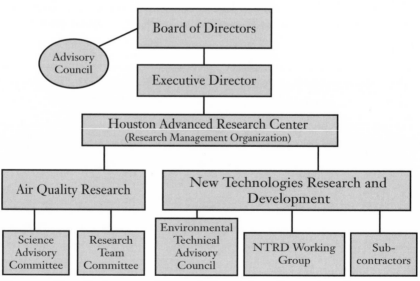

Figure 15. Texas Environmental Research Consortium. (Source: http://www .tercairquality.org)

makers, composed of six county judges, the mayors of Dallas and Houston, and a representative of the Environmental Defense Fund. The organization receives funding from both the state and federal governments. The bulk of funds are spent on contracts with Texas universities, nonprofit organizations, and corporations. Two kinds of projects are supported: research on regional air quality, with a contract volume of about 3 million dollars per year; and research on new environmental technologies, with a contract volume of about 8 million dollars per year (see Figure 15).

Initially the consortium focused on Houston and East Texas. The Dallas–Fort Worth metroplex has since been included. The two cities are home to more than 10 million people. They face a pressing deadline to meet the national air-quality standard for ground-level ozone. Research results obtained so far play an important role in improving air-quality regulations for Texas. The new Technology Research and Development Program funds projects aimed at helping commercialize innovative technologies to cut ozone-forming nitrogen oxide from diesel engines, the dominant source of nitrogen oxide.[8]

Over the last four years TERC has administered over 10 million dollars in research funds aimed at improving emissions inventories, air-quality modeling and monitoring, and air regulations and policy. HARC plays a pivotal role as TERC's research management organization. As such, HARC issues requests for proposals, advises TERC's board on contract selection, synthesizes research results, and develops policy recommendations.

CHAPTER 10

The Mitchell Paradox

Mitchell's half-century commitment to sustainability had yielded important results: The Woodlands, a community designed with nature; the Woodlands Conferences and the Mitchell Prize, dedicated to defining the nature of a sustainable society; the Mitchell Center, studying the regional impacts of global change; the National Academy of Sciences, defining the role of science in sustainable development; and the new HARC, focused on linking regional sustainability to sustainability science. In this chapter we look at whether sustainability also became a guiding principle in other parts of Mitchell's career.

Early on, Mitchell had closely followed the emerging environmental debate, from Rachel Carson's book *Silent Spring* in the sixties to the 1978 crisis at Love Canal, New York, where drinking water had been contaminated by a toxic waste site. As a resident of Houston, Mitchell joined a coalition of residents and environmental activists who protested the practice of cementing the banks of Houston's bayous as a means of controlling flooding. His work in oil and gas led him to read widely about waste and pollution problems caused by the energy industry. He felt that business people eventually responded to these dangers but often waited too long. His core conviction was shaped in the 1970s: "Efforts to solve environmental issues are very important.... Yet it's not enough. Sustainability is a much bigger issue. Environmentalists should think one notch higher than what they are doing.... They need to convert the environmental interest into sustainability interest."[1]

This statement, which Mitchell repeated over and over again in various forms, would lead one to expect that the pursuit of sustainability would permeate all aspects of his life. Yet in many ways, this was not the case. At Mitchell Energy and Development, he followed standard industrial practices. He obeyed the law and made adjustments as stricter governmental regulations for the oil and gas industry came on line. At times, when acting environmentally did not hurt the business, he would go further. "We as a company worked on the idea of being environmentally responsible as the major step toward sustainability.... We worked with EPA on drilling wells, where we would support things that helped EPA do it right."[2]

In one of his gas fields Mitchell set aside land for protection of the endangered whooping crane. In another case, "we abandoned a field offshore and put the platform in the seabed to make a reef for the fish. It cost us 500,000 dollars to do that, but we saved 300,000 dollars by not plugging out the wells the regular way."[3] MND stockholders and staff supported environmentally friendly projects, and the company got good publicity out of them. But the company never made environmental causes or sustainability an explicit part of its mission. Nor did Mitchell look at environmental experience in hiring staff or train employees in the sustainable management of oil and gas. While Mitchell risked his reputation and fortune by building a green city, he never changed MND into a green company.

One of his children calls this the Mitchell paradox. Involved in a half-century-long intellectual pursuit to characterize the forces that threaten the carrying capacity of the earth, Mitchell employed philanthropy and persuasion to motivate others to pursue sustainability solutions. Yet his personal actions were often less progressive than the positions he advocated. Two conferences at The Woodlands were devoted to efforts by business leaders who transformed their companies to lessen their environmental footprint, yet corporate sustainability was not promoted as a core value at Mitchell Energy and Development Corporation.

The real estate developments executed by The Woodlands Corporation are recognized for their adherence to the "design with nature" philosophy, but many environmental advocates felt that nature itself was preferable. Some critics saw the development of a new town of 130,000 people in the forested exurbs of Houston as a continuation of the sprawl that plagued Houston. Mitchell faced environmental opposition in Galveston for building second-home subdivisions on the fringe of Galveston Bay wetlands, and in Aspen, Colorado, for his attempt to develop a ski area in the Owl Creek valley where preservation of wildlife habitat and a rural landscape were preferred by local regulators. Although his company's real estate projects have been praised for their commitment to environmental design, Mitchell was no stranger to conflict with environmental activists.

Mitchell's positions regarding the environmental impacts of fossil fuel extraction highlight the paradox. While a long-time advocate of the environmental benefits of natural gas as an alternative to more polluting fossil fuels, Mitchell has struggled with his beliefs about the role of anthropogenic carbon dioxide emissions as a cause for the modern increase in global temperatures. In that debate, he has often taken the view, informed by his background in geology, that climate variations are natural cycles that predate the advent of industrialization. Only recently has Mitchell conceded that fossil fuel emissions may be a contributing factor to global warming, but he insists that the impacts may be less than predicted by the scientific community.

So what is to be made of this paradox, an industrialist who has become a leading advocate of environmental sustainability while himself being a product of two industries—fossil fuel extraction and real estate development— that are often in the crosshairs of environmental activists?

Whatever else can be said about Mitchell, his friends and colleagues would say that he is a man who is guided by ideas and is unafraid to pursue an intellectual path that points to his own contradictions. Robert Harriss, president of the Houston Advanced Research Center, remembers a telephone call from Mitchell asking for a briefing on the human contribution to climate change. With a research career in atmospheric chemistry, Harriss was able to summarize the scientific consensus on the human contribution to global warming, and it was after their meeting that Mitchell began to shift in his views on climate change. Yet Mitchell's uncertainty about carbon dioxide emissions and climate change never affected his philanthropy. Mitchell was always unafraid to be a catalyst, providing resources and intellectual stimulus to ask difficult questions, even if the answers challenged his own long-held assumptions about the role of human society and nature.

In his real estate development career, Mitchell saw nature in terms of human utility, and therefore saw no contradiction in converting a natural landscape into one to be enjoyed by people. But he did so with a reasonable commitment to preserving as much wilderness as possible. He was willing to create tension in his real estate development teams between the civil engineers and sales people on the one hand—those who had to build and market a parcel of land—and the environmental designers on the other hand, whose passion was to create a new kind of urbanization, preserving as many of the natural assets as possible.

Mitchell often found himself on the right side of history, and The Woodlands is an example. In a metropolitan region famed for its lack of zoning and planning, urban sprawl has in fact consumed the northern reaches of the city and moved steadily into Montgomery County where The Woodlands is located. Seen from an airplane, The Woodlands is an island of green, albeit developed with homes and businesses, in what is otherwise a bleak landscape of concrete, strip centers, and stamped-out residential neighborhoods. If urban sprawl was inevitable, then at least The Woodlands serves as an example of urban design that leaves green space and watersheds reasonably intact.

In the energy policy debate, Mitchell also finds himself today in the mainstream of energy policy that advocates a transition to low-carbon energy sources. While undecided on his views on carbon emissions and climate change, Mitchell nonetheless has for decades touted natural gas as a cleaner fuel than coal and oil alternatives. His advocacy of natural gas for electrical power generation was spurred by the mandates of the Clean Air Act in the 1970s; the relatively lower emissions of particulates and sulfur and nitrogen compounds, as compared to coal, positioned gas as the obvious winner in an emissions-oriented regulatory environment. When tight gas supplies and price volatility in the 1990s caused utilities and policy makers to fear that natural gas was a costly and unreliable fuel, Mitchell lobbied for recognition that the natural gas resource base in the United States was far larger than most policy makers understood, and that a policy to accelerate development of the resource was in the nation's interest.

But Mitchell did more than just engage in policy debate. He bet his company's future on technical innovations to produce natural gas from black shales that were previously thought to be unproductive. The engineering approach pioneered at Mitchell Energy is now used in black shale plays around the world. As a result, natural gas supplies that are more abundant than previously understood represent an opportunity to reduce greenhouse gas emissions. Moreover, natural gas power plants are considered to be ideal as backup power generation for wind farms because their construction costs are relatively low and they can quickly bring power online to smooth out the intermittent power of wind.

Still, some people have been highly critical of MND's environmental record. Several property owners living close to the company's gas fields in North Texas believed that drilling operations had damaged their water wells and thereby polluted the environment. They brought suit against the company, which was initially successful. The company was fined an enormous amount—204 million dollars, which at the time were the highest amount of punitive damages awarded in the state for groundwater contamination. On appeal, after Mitchell had spent 37 million dollars in legal costs, the verdict was overturned.

No stranger to controversy, Mitchell's engagement with sustainability was sometimes as contradictory as it was committed. He was concerned about overpopulation but had ten children. He believed in clean energy but with a businessman's point of view. He promoted natural spaces but with a developer's mindset. This paradox speaks to the complexity not only of human beings but of the issue of sustainability in a world soon populated by 9 billion people, which Mitchell has tried to make more sustainable—in one way or another—throughout his life.

Mitchell, as we have seen, worked relentlessly to advance understanding of sustainability and its incorporation in the national agenda. He used a substantial part of his fortune and energy to advance these goals. He also risked his reputation and the future of his energy company in building The Woodlands as a green city. As I discussed in chapter 1, Mitchell Energy and Development focused on natural gas as a cleaner energy source than coal and oil, and twenty years before Mitchell sold the company, began to revolutionize the extraction of natural gas. By so doing he opened the door to a significant reduction in carbon dioxide emissions from power plants. In the end, therefore, Mitchell promoted sustainability in several ways: he worked relentlessly as a philanthropist and advocate but also transformed the energy business by making natural gas available as a relatively clean bridge fuel on the way to a sustainable, noncarbon energy future.

CHAPTER 11

Mitchell's Impact and Legacy

George Mitchell's faith in sustainability as the guiding principle for future development remains as strong as ever. In an April 2006 interview he said: "We have seen a tremendous interest in environmental issues all over the world. We are going to have the same interest, only on a much larger scale, in thinking about sustainability over the next twenty-five to fifty years."[1] Over the years, many of his business acquaintances praised him for his success in oil and gas and in building a new town. Yet often they would ask: "You are so busy, why do you bother about sustainability?" Mitchell's standard answer has not changed over the years: "Because it's a serious problem, and you are going to find out some day it is."[2]

In all, seven Woodlands Conferences, each dedicated to an important aspect of sustainable development, were held between 1975 and 2001. There is no other conference series, in the United States or elsewhere, that offered a similar opportunity for scholars and decision makers to explore the nature of sustainability over the course of twenty-five years. The scope of papers and discussions broadened over time: At first, the Club of Rome's call for limits to growth was brought to an American audience. George Mitchell then pushed for consideration of "good" versus "bad" growth. This distinction became central in exploring the characteristics and management of sustainable societies. Reflecting Mitchell's interest, two conferences, twenty years apart, examined the role of private enterprise in building sustainable societies. Another conference was devoted to discussion of climate change and ways to cope with this threat to sustainability. And one conference focused on the transition to sustainability—the period of the next fifty years during which sustainability in food, energy, and consumption has to be achieved. Each conference, in addition, was the occasion to award the International Mitchell Prize for Sustainable Development to scientists, political leaders, and corporate executives.

As noted previously, the Woodlands Conferences have not yielded significant comment in the published literature on sustainable development. This oversight needs to be corrected. My research shows that envisioning a sustainable society, which is the very keystone of the sustainability movement, first occurred at the 1977 Woodlands conference. Taken together, the conferences, the Mitchell Prize, and Mitchell's initiatives at HARC and the National Academies had a large but rarely recognized impact that encouraged, supported, and validated the work of emerging leaders in the sustainability field. Many of these individuals have gone on to tackle important issues and influence countless individuals and institutions. Mitchell's sustainability initiatives will continue to enrich the intellectual framework of the next generation of scholars and policy makers.

The following quotes illustrate the impact the Mitchell Prize had on selected recipients:

> The prize supported our confidence and the resulting activities did help to develop an international network.
>
> —Harrie Eijkelhof, Senior Scholar, 1977

> It was a factor in my appointment as General Manager of Spirax Sarco Japan in 1982. Spirax is a world leader in energy-saving steam systems.
>
> —Andrew Michael Gamble, Senior Scholar, 1977

> [The Mitchell Prize] achieved the basic goals needed to make a difference: bringing individualists, thinkers, and visionaries in a variety of related fields together with a common aim; encouraging discourse and collaboration; creating credibility of the subject matter and providing such to the individual scientists/thinkers for their work; ensuring proper records and information dissemination.
>
> —David Hopcraft, Senior Scholar, 1979

> I think it was seminal work but not taken seriously because the time was not yet ripe. Revisiting this body of work now through a series of lectures, reprints, a new book, etc., would be a very productive project for George if he still wants to have an impact.
>
> —William E. Halal, Senior Scholar, 1977

Having won the Mitchell Prize influenced my career afterward, when
I decided to organize the ICID (International Conference on Sustainable Development) and Climate Variations in Semiarid Regions and the
Aridas Project, a strategy for sustainable development of the semiarid
Northeast region of Brazil.

—Antônio Magalhães, Senior Scholar, 1991

I have been a world leader in moving adaptation up the international
agenda both in IPCC (share of the Nobel Prize) and in UNFCCC.

—Ian Burton, Senior Scholar, 1991

[Receiving the Mitchell Prize was] very important. It was a great benefit.
It meant much to me personally to be so recognized, and this encouraged
me to continue on with my work. Since the work I was doing (and still do)
tends to be controversial, this was important.

—Daniel Botkin, Senior Scholar, 1991

The perspectives I took home from the Woodlands Conference shaped
all my future research and writing.... Though an English professor, I
coordinate our university's Environmental Studies Minor.

—W. John Coletta, Senior Scholar, 1979

I eventually cofounded the Sustainability Council of Ventura County in
1996 and led it for eight years, fulfilling my Mitchell Prize mission. It is
still in existence.

—Robert Chianese, Senior Scholar, 1979

[The] Mitchell Prize for Young Scholars was important for me as a
confirmation that I can do something good in bridging the gaps between
scientific research and policy-relevant understanding of global environmental issues.

—Georgii Alexandrov, Young Scholar, 1991

The meeting helped me to meet other researchers working on climate
change research, and this network-building among researchers from dif-

ferent disciplines working on climate change has been very important in
the years since then.

—Karen O'Brien, Young Scholar, 1991

The research formed the foundation for an ongoing research agenda and
further projects undertaken with Justin Keeble, including work for the
UK government's Sustainable Consumption and Production Programme
in 2005–2006.

—Jason Chilvers, Young Scholar, 2001

It was reaffirming to meet some people in the United States who knew
my work. It meant it wasn't just UK and Western Europe that were "getting it." It made me think that doing this work could also be fun at times,
as I would be congratulated. That was new.

—Jem Bendell, Young Scholar, 2001

It was a recognition that boosted confidence and focused my research
thinking.

—Young Scholar, 2001

At the time of this writing, Mitchell and his children and grandchildren are
planning how they will continue his work on sustainability into the future. At
the center of this effort is the Cynthia and George Mitchell Foundation. In
Mitchell's own words: "The foundation has an important role. It might coordinate with what HARC is doing, and try to work with the National Academy
of Sciences."[3] Frank Press, with whom Mitchell had negotiated the initial
collaboration with the National Academy of Sciences, commented: "I think
that's a remarkable thing to do.... There are very few businessmen ... or
women, especially from his area of the business sector, that are so involved.
So he's setting a standard there that I hope will be emulated by [others]."[4]
The foundation is supporting a program on clean energy as its first priority.
A second program is likely to focus on water. Other aspects of sustainability
will be included in the future. Mitchell also took several actions to support
continued work on sustainability science at the National Academies as well as
at HARC.

For Mitchell, *Our Common Journey* was the beginning of a long-term relationship with the National Academy of Sciences. Once the project had been
completed to his satisfaction, Mitchell proposed to support a large Academy
initiative that would span several decades. "I don't want to put my money in
a three- or four-year program. It's a long-term problem," and must be addressed over many years.[5] Responding to this invitation the Academy agreed
to build a long-term program dedicated to sustainability. With that promise in hand, Mitchell created the George and Cynthia Mitchell Endowment
for Sustainability Science at the National Academy of Sciences. In 2002 he
pledged 10 million dollars, with the possibility of matching up to another
10 million dollars if the Academy reached certain outside funding goals for
sustainability-related projects, whether funded by private donations or project grants from federal agencies. To encourage the Academy to use this gift as
leverage for others to give as well, Mitchell designed the "Mitchell match":
the Academy first had to raise 10 million dollars in sustainability-related programs to get to a level point with the initial gift, and then he would match up
to an additional 10 million dollars depending on what had been raised within
the next four and a half years. While this outside funding could be used to pay
for current financial needs of new projects, the Mitchell funds have to be used
exclusively as a long-term endowment. Well before the cutoff date, the Academies as of March 1, 2006, had initiated forty-three sustainability projects
and had already received almost 23 million dollars, with anticipated overall
funding to exceed 38 million dollars. The largest single contribution to the
program fund was made by the Bill and Melinda Gates Foundation, of which
3.5 million dollars was counted towards the Mitchell match.

With the help of Mitchell's grant, the National Academy of Sciences is
building an ongoing project on sustainability science. This is an innovative
step for the Academy. As Bruce Alberts explained in an interview, the traditional role of the Academy has been to review and evaluate the completed
work of other scientists and organizations. Now it is much more in the role
of initiating and conducting studies on sustainability. To manage these activities, a Science and Technology for Sustainability Program has been established in the division of Policy and Global Affairs. To guide the work of the
new program the Academies have convened the Roundtable on Science and
Technology for Sustainability. Roundtable membership includes leaders from

government, business, nongovernmental organizations, and universities. Pamela Matson and Bill Clark, members of the team that produced *Our Common* Journey, are actively involved and ensure continuity with the original work on sustainability science. Discussions among members of the roundtable generate plans for the Academy's sustainability projects. Three goals are being pursued. First, the roundtable will focus on strategic needs and opportunities for science and technology to contribute to the transition toward sustainability. Second, the roundtable will focus on issues for which progress requires cooperation among multiple sectors, including academia, government (at all levels), business, nongovernmental organizations, and international institutions. Third, the roundtable will focus on activities where scientific knowledge and technology can help to advance practices that contribute directly to sustainability goals, in addition to identifying priorities for research and development inspired by sustainability challenges.[6]

Ralph Cicerone, another member of the Board on Sustainable Development, has taken over the presidency of the Academy. He follows his predecessors, Press and Alberts, in giving high priority and visibility to the work on sustainability. He describes the ongoing work as follows: "We are considering several new activities in sustainability that will marshal the resources of all of the committees and boards and study groups that are looking at individual issues, such as radioactive waste management or mineral resources, energy, science and technology and energy policy, medical issues in the Third World, educational issues in the Third World. Our job is to bring all this together. And it is very difficult, but it's also a very positive challenge. We're extremely happy to have the opportunity."[7] In this vein, the Academy hosts a network for "Emerging Leaders in Sustainability" and publishes a special section of its *Proceedings of the National Academy of Sciences* on sustainability science. Mitchell has noted: "All the other academies of the world have asked our academy to lead the way to sustainability. So the National Academy has a major role to invigorate our nation [about sustainability] but also to get the other academies to be concerned about it and get their nations to be concerned about it."[8]

Mitchell discussed plans to continue the Mitchell Prize with the National Academies. In these discussions "it was brought up that the Nobel Foundation is thinking about a prize on sustainability. That would be the most important of all things that could be done. I suggested that the Academy find out more about that and how they may be able to work with them. We and others in the private sector could help them get funding for it."[9] Yet the preferred option did not work—the Nobel committee signaled continued discomfort with its prize for economics and unwillingness to add another "soft" prize. Mitchell has not given up: "We'll regroup and discuss with the National Academy if we do something else about a prize."[10]

In Texas in 2005, Mitchell established the Endowment for Regional Sustainability Science, a private foundation to which he deeded stock initially valued at 25 million dollars. In 2007 the endowment signed a grant agreement with HARC. Income from this endowment gives HARC the long-term stability to pursue its mission to conduct projects in support of regional sustainability. Mitchell said: "My dream is that HARC will always stand as a gateway to scientific discovery and performance."

Robert Harriss, HARC's president since 2006, sees HARC serving Mitchell's sustainability vision by following three general strategies. The first strategy is building productive partnerships and networks with university partners, decision makers in both the public and private sectors, and the public at large. It is becoming well established that industrial era "top down" solutions have a much higher failure rate than "integrative and adaptive" approaches that engage all interested parties. The second strategy is tapping into talent and finding ways of using increased connections to nurture, sustain, attract, and promote talent, wherever it may reside. The future of innovation and competitiveness will belong to regions and nations that can most effectively attract and cultivate brainpower. The third strategy is to acknowledge that creativity and innovation will be essential to the future prosperity of the Houston region and the nation.

Mitchell's search for a sustainable society, pursued incessantly over the course of half a century, spans a wide range. As founder of a Fortune 500 energy company, he pioneered the use of natural gas as a less carbon-intensive bridge fuel on the way to a less carbon-intensive economy. As a real estate developer he demonstrated how to build a new community with respect for nature. As a philanthropist he created ongoing initiatives in support of sustainability science and sustainability planning. His legacy continues at Devon Energy, The Woodlands, the National Academy of Sciences, the Houston Advanced Research Center, and the Mitchell Family Foundation. And it lives on in other places, as illustrated eloquently by Dean Pamela Matson in her comment on changes brought to Stanford University as a result of Mitchell's Academy project: "We have worked very hard to harness the strengths that we have throughout the university … around sustainability. I feel incredibly lucky to have been part of that whole thing. It changed my life."[11]

Laureates of the International George and Cynthia Mitchell Prize for Sustainable Development

The Mitchell Prize was awarded to several individuals in 1975, 1977, 1979, 1982, and 1991. The selection was based on an open essay competition in which the prizewinners prepared an essay on some aspect of sustainability and a panel of judges ranked abstracts and full papers. In the following list I include abstracts of three prizewinning essays that I view as particularly important.

In 1997 and 2001 the Mitchell Prize was awarded to a single individual for outstanding professional performance in the field of sustainability. Candidates were recommended by a committee convened by the National Academy of Sciences.

The Young Scholars Award was given in 1991, 1997, and 2001. In each of these years, up to ten individuals under the age of thirty-five received the prize for an outstanding work plan on some aspect of sustainability. The young scholars met again in the following year to report on the results of their project.

1975
Limits to Growth '75: The First Biennial Assessment of Alternatives to Growth
Bruce Hannon, University of Illinois, Urbana, Illinois (First Prize)
"Economic Growth, Energy Use, and Altruism"

Robert Allen, International Union for Conservation of Nature and Natural Resources, Morges, Switzerland (Second Prize)
"Toward a Primary Lifestyle"

John Tanton, Zero Population Growth, Petoskey, Michigan (Third Prize)
"International Migration and World Stability"

Joan Davis and Samuel Mauch, Zurich, Switzerland (Fourth Prize)
"Strategies for Societal Development"

1977
Alternatives to Growth '77: The Nature of Growth in Equitable and Sustainable Societies

Andrew Michael Gamble, University of Sheffield, England, and David Earle Gamble, Barlow International Services, London, England
"Towards a Sustainable State Economy in the United Kingdom"

William E. Halal, American University, Washington, D.C.
"Beyond the Profit Motive: The Postindustrial Corporation"

Jerome M. Weingart, International Institute for Applied Systems Analysis, Laxenburg, Austria
"The Helios Strategy—A Heretical View of the Role of Solar Energy in the Future of a Small Planet"

Charles J. Ryan, Massachusetts Institute of Technology, Cambridge, Massachusetts
"The Choices in the Next Energy and Social Revolution"

Egbert Boeker, Ministry of Science Policy, The Hague, Netherlands, and Harrie Eijkelhof, Free University of Amsterdam, Netherlands
"Alternatives to Growth in Education—A Course on 'Physics and Society' in Dutch Secondary Education"

1979
The Management of Sustainable Growth

Paul R. Ehrlich, Stanford University, Palo Alto, California (First Prize)
"Diversity and the Steady State"

> *Abstract.* The diversity of nonhuman organisms and the genetic, cultural, and technological diversity of our own species are crucial to the future health, happiness, and perhaps even survival of humanity.

Therefore, those concerned with planning for a transition from today's growth-oriented society to a society that might persist over the long term must give careful consideration to the roles played by various kinds of diversity in human affairs, how diversity can be maintained, and how diversity can be regenerated once it has been lost. This essay attempts to provide a starting point for such consideration.

Robert L. Chianese, California State University, Northridge, California
"New Metaphors, Myths, and Values for a Steady State Future"

Edward T. Clark Jr. and W. John Coletta, George Williams College, Downers Grove, Illinois
"Ecosystem Education: A Strategy for Social Change"

Arthur A. Few Jr., Rice University, Houston, Texas
"Social, Environmental, and Economic Implications of Widespread Conversion to Biomass-based Fuels"

James Garbarino, Center for the Study of Youth Development, Boys Town, Omaha, Nebraska
"The Issue is Human Quality: In Praise of Children"

Michael Gibbons, University of Manchester, England
"Some Implications of Low Economic Growth Rates for the Development of Science and Technology in the United Kingdom"

David Hopcraft, Game Ranching, Ltd., Nairobi, Kenya
"Nature's Technology"

George Modelski, University of Washington, Seattle, Washington
"World Politics and Sustainable Growth: A Structural Model of the World System"

Dillard B. Tinsley, Stephen F. Austin State University, Nacogdoches, Texas
"Business Organizations in the Sustainable Society"

1982
The Future and the Private Sector

Orville Freeman and Ruth Karen, Business International Corporation, New York City (First Prize)

"The Farmer and the Money Economy: Role of the Private Sector in Agricultural Development of LDCS"

Abstract. The world's food/people balance is precarious now and will become more precarious in the future, both in terms of supply and price. The grain-producing industrial countries have come close to reaching their production potential. The solution lies in exploiting the production capacity of the developing world. At present only half of the world's good arable land is being farmed. Most of the other half does not have the necessary infrastructure, and opening it up to cultivation will require major capital investment. This means that a serious political commitment is required, primarily by LDC governments. There are concomitants for aid policy as well. The key action-oriented question is where, and how, productivity increase can take place. The authors suggest that the most effective method requires involvement of the private sector, specifically the participation of small landholders, working 1–5 acres, grouped around a corporate core. The corporate core provides technical, educational, and financial inputs, and processes and/or markets the output. In a widening circle of socioeconomic benefits, work can be offered to landless peasants, and both the farmer and the peasant are brought into the money economy with the overall developmental dynamic this implies.

Armory B. Lovins and L. Hunter Lovins, independent consultants on Energy Policy, Snowmass, Colorado (Second Prize)
"Electric Utilities: Key to Capitalizing the Energy Transition"

Charles Kiefer, Innovation Associates, and Peter Senge, Massachusetts Institute of Technology, Cambridge, Massachusetts (Third Prize)
"Metanoic Organizations in the Transition to a Sustainable Society"

Walter R. Stahel, Speno International, Geneva, Switzerland (Third Prize)
"The Product-Life Factor"

M. Perry Chapman, professional planner, Watertown, Massachusetts
"The Mature Region: Building a Practical Model for the Transition to the Sustainable Society"

Ann C. Crouter and James Garbarino, Pennsylvania State University, University Park, Pennsylvania
"Corporate Self-Reliance and the Sustainable Society"

Jeanmarie K. Heller, University of Wisconsin, Milwaukee
"Intercultural Communication: Necessary for International Corporations and Sustainable Societies"

Arthur C. Miller, former legal consultant to Senate Watergate Committee, Key West, Florida
"Constitutionalizing the Corporation"

John Nicholls, consultant, Geneva, Switzerland
"Towards a Sustainable Society: The Private Sector in Six Guises"

Matthias von Oppen, International Crops Research Institute for the Semi-arid Tropics, Andhra Pradesh, India
"Toward Private Investment Funds for Development Aid"

1991
The Regions and Global Warming
Senior Prize
Daniel Botkin, University of California, Santa Barbara, California (First Prize)
"Global Warming and Forests of the Great Lake States: An Example of the Use of Quantitative Projections in Policy Analysis"

Abstract. Computer models of forest growth, developed by the author and described in this paper, project that global warming will lead to rapid and severe changes in forests of the Great Lakes states, with some areas suffering major diebacks during the first decades of the twenty-first century and some becoming deforested and unable to support trees by the end of that century. Without careful preparation and planning, severe economic disruptions will occur in forestry and the production of forest products, major industries of the region. In addition, recreation, aesthetics, and biological conservation will suffer; presently endangered species many be threatened with extinction. A business-as-usual approach to environmental policy, one that assumes that biological resources are sustainable through a simple, constant rate of harvest that ignores environmental variability, cannot hope to succeed.

A new approach, combining realistic computer models within a new perspective on nature, is illustrated in this paper for the Great Lakes region. This approach gives insight into a range of issues, from how a forester motivated simply to maximize his timber yield might harvest forests under global warming, to ways to set priorities for land-use allocation. The analysis for the Great Lakes region presented in this paper provides a basis for development of realistic environmental policies under global warming for other regions of the world.

José Goldemberg, Ministry of Science and Technology, São Paulo, Brazil (Second Prize)
"Global Climate Change: What Can Developing Countries Do?"

Diana Liverman, Pennsylvania State University, University Park, Pennsylvania (Second Prize)
"The Regional Impact of Global Warming in Mexico: Uncertainty, Vulnerability, and Response"

Ian Burton, International Federation of Institutes for Advanced Study, Toronto, Canada (Third Prize)
"Regions of Resilience: An Essay on Global Warming"

Michael Glantz, National Center for Atmospheric Research, Boulder, Colorado (Third Prize)
"The Use of Analogies in Assessing Physical and Societal Responses to Global Warming"

Antônio R. Magalhães, Government of Ceará, Brasilia, Distrito Federal, Brazil (Third Prize)
"Understanding the Implications of Global Warming in Developing Regions: The Case of Northeast Brazil"

William Moomaw, Tufts University, Medford, Massachusetts (Third Prize)
"Regional Boundaries and Global Climate Change: Northeast North America"

Vijaya Ruby Saha, Ministry of Housing, Lands, and the Environment, Port Louis, Mauritius (Third Prize)
"Climate Change—Need for National Awareness and Commitment among Small Regional Communities: The Case of the Southwest Indian Ocean Islands"

Young Scholars Award
Amrita N. Achanta, Tata Energy Research Institute, New Delhi, India
"Potential Impacts of Global Warming on Indian Rice Production"

Georgii A. Alexandrov, Computing Center of the USSR Academy of Sciences, Moscow, USSR
"Raised Mire Response to Climate Change: An Expert System Based on Outcomes of a Simulation Model"

John Antonov, State Hydrological Institute, Leningrad, USSR
"Ecological, Climatic and Economic Aspects of the Caspian-Aral Tragedy: A Step to Future "Science-Policy" Dialogue"

Gordon B. Bonan, National Center for Atmospheric Research, Boulder, Colorado
"Atmosphere-Biosphere Exchange for CO_2 in Boreal Forests: A Potential Global Change Feedback"

F. Brian Dilley, Pennsylvania State University, University Park, Pennsylvania
"The Meaning of Global Climate Change for Peasant Farmers in the Oaxaca Valley of Mexico"

Bruce Hewitson, Pennsylvania State University, University Park, Pennsylvania
"Regional Climate Change Prediction in General Circulation Models"

Karen L. O'Brien, Pennsylvania State University, University Park,
Pennsylvania
"Global Change and Biodiversity: The Case of Deforestation in Mexico"

Peter J. Poole, Massachusetts Institute of Technology, and National Institute for Environmental Studies, Tsukuba, Japan
"Technology Offers the Answer: Japanese Management of the Risks of the Greenhouse Effect"

Deborah D. Stine, National Academy of Sciences, Washington, D.C.
"International Environmental Decision Making"

Alexey A. Vionov, Computing Center of the USSR Academy of Sciences,
Moscow, USSR
"Impacts of Global Climatic Change on Freshwater Ecosystems"

1997
Sustainable Development: Managing the Transition
Lifetime Achievement Award
Marcelo C. de Andrade, Chairman and Founder, Pro-Natura, Rio de Janeiro
and New York City

Young Scholars Award
Jayesh Bhatia, Tata Energy Research Institute, New Delhi, India
"Industry-Farmer Linkage for the Paper and Pulp Industry in India"

Christopher J. Carr, Washburn, and Briscoe McCarthy, San Francisco,
California
"Making the Transition to Sustainable Fisheries: New Technology for Regulators and Fishermen"

Elizabeth Conover, Stapleton Development Corporation, Denver, Colorado
"Changing the Way Cities Are Made: The Stapleton Development Project"

Pierre Desrochers, University of Montreal, Canada
"How Would the Invisible Hand Handle Solid Waste?"

Alastair Iles, Harvard University, Cambridge, Massachusetts
"Fostering Social Learning in Industrial Firms for Sustainable
Development"

Katrina Smith Korfmacher, Denison University, Granville, Ohio
"Planning for Sustainability: Preservation of Agricultural Resources in Lick-
ing County, Ohio"

Mitchell L. Mathis, University of Texas, Austin
"Market Mechanisms for the Efficient Allocation of Water Resources: A
Study of Tradable Water Rights and the Emergence of Water Markets in
Semiarid Regions"

Laszlo Pinter, International Institute for Sustainable Development, Win-
nipeg, Canada
"Think Public, Act Private: Building Compatibility between Corporate and
Public Visions of Sustainable Development"

Andrew Seidl, CPAP/EMBRAPA, Corumba, Brazil
"A Spatial Economic Analysis of Deforestation for Cultivated Pastures on
Sustainable Development in the Brazilian Pantanal"

2001
Corporate Capabilities and Tools: Making Sustainability Work in the
Twenty-first Century
Lifetime Achievement Award
Ray C. Anderson, Founder and Chairman, Interface, Inc., Atlanta, Georgia

Young Scholars Award
Jem Bendell, University of Bristol, United Kingdom
"Finding Banana Karma: The Role of Civil Society in Chiquita's Conversion
to Sustainability"

Hilary Bradbury, Case Western Reserve University, Cleveland, Ohio
"The Greening of Identity, Commitment, and Purpose: The Case of Xerox LAKES"

Jason D. Chilvers, University College, London, and Justin J. Keeble, Arthur D. Little, United Kingdom
"Corporate Incentives and the Dynamics of Environmental Decision-making: An In-depth Study of Dudley UK Ltd."

Panagiotis Karamanos, Duke University, Durham, North Carolina
"Entergy Energy Company and Voluntary Sustainable Business Practices"

Monica Kearns, National Conference of State Legislatures, Denver, Colorado, and Andrea Ramage, CH2M HILL, Inc., Bellevue, Washington
"Drivers for Sustainable Business Practices: A Case Study of CH2M Hill"

Mark B. Milstein, University of North Carolina–Chapel Hill
"Freeplay Energy Group"

Marlo A. Raynolds, Pembina Institute for Appropriate Development, Calgary, Alberta, Canada
"Suncor Energy, Inc."

Nosiku Sipilanymbe, Royal Institute of Technology, Stockholm, Sweden
"Corporations and Sustainability: A Case Study of Zambia Electricity Supply Corporation"

Vesela R. Veleva, University of Massachusetts–Lowell
"Stonyfield Farm: The Business Model for Social and Environmental Responsibility"

Frank Wijen, Tilburg University, Netherlands
"The Quest for Sustainability: The Case of the 'Greenheart' Company"

Conferences Sponsored by George P. Mitchell

1974 First Woodlands Conference: Limits to Growth—The First Bi-
      ennial Assessment of Alternatives to Growth
1977 Second Woodlands Conference: Alternatives to Growth (The Na-
      ture of Growth in Equitable and Sustainable Societies)
1979 Third Woodlands Conference: The Management of Sustainable
      Growth
1982 Fourth Woodlands Conference: The Future and the Private Sector
1985 Technology Transfer: U.S.-Mexico Perspectives
1987 Mexican and Central American Population and U.S. Immigration
      Policy
1988 New State Roles: Environment, Resources, and the Economy
1989 U.S.-Mexico Industrial Integration
1991 Fifth Woodlands Conference: The Regions and Global Warming
1992 Mitchell Prize Laureates Workshop of Senior and Young Scholars
1994 Uniting the Basin: The Rio Grande/Río Bravo Sustainable Devel-
      opment Conference
1997 Sixth Woodlands Conference: Sustainable Development—Manag-
      ing the Transition
2001 Seventh Woodlands Conference: Corporate Capabilities and
      Tools—Making Sustainability Work in the Twenty-first Century

APPENDIX 3

Conference Proceedings, Books, and Reports from the Woodlands Conferences and the Mitchell Center

Conference Proceedings

1975 Woodlands Conference and Mitchell Prize competition
Alternatives to Growth I: A Search for Sustainable Futures, edited by Dennis Meadows. Cambridge, Mass.: Ballinger Publishing Co., 1977.

1977 Woodlands Conference and Mitchell Prize competition
An Inquiry into the Nature of Sustainable Societies: Alternatives to Growth, edited by Susan Grinton Orr. Mimeographed. The Woodlands, Tex.: Center for Growth Studies, Houston Advanced Research Center, 1984. [Papers of 1977 Mitchell Prize winners]

1979 Woodlands Conference and Mitchell Prize competition
Quest for a Sustainable Society, edited by James C. Coomer. University of Houston, Clear Lake. Elmsford, N.Y.: Pergamon Press, 1981. [Papers of the 1979 Mitchell Prize winners]

The Management of Sustainable Growth, edited by Harlan Cleveland. Elmsford, N.Y.: Pergamon Press, 1981. [Commissioned papers]

1982 Woodlands Conference and Mitchell Prize competition
An Inquiry into the Nature of Sustainable Societies: The Role of the Private Sector, edited by Susan Grinton Orr. Mimeographed. The Woodlands, Tex.: Center for Growth Studies, Houston Advanced Research Center, 1984. [Papers of the 1982 Mitchell Prize winners]

1988 CONFERENCE
New State Roles: Environment, Resources, and the Economy, edited by Jurgen Schmandt. Mimeographed. The Woodlands, Tex.: Center for Growth Studies, Houston Advanced Research Center, 1988. [Background papers]

1989 CONFERENCE
Mexico and Central American Population and U.S. Immigration Policy, edited by Frank Bean, Jurgen Schmandt, and Sidney Weintraub. Austin: Center for Mexican American Studies, University of Texas, 1989.

1990 CONFERENCE
U.S.-Mexico Industrial Integration: The Road to Free Trade, edited by Sidney Weintraub, Luis Rubio, and Alan D. Jones. Boulder, Colo.: Westview Press, 1991.

1991 WOODLANDS CONFERENCE AND MITCHELL PRIZE COMPETITION
The Regions and Global Warming: Impacts and Response Strategies, edited by Jurgen Schmandt and Judith Clarkson. New York: Oxford University Press, 1992.

1997 WOODLANDS CONFERENCE AND MITCHELL PRIZE COMPETITION
Sustainable Development: The Challenge of Transition, edited by Jurgen Schmandt and C. H. Ward. Cambridge: Cambridge University Press, 1998.

2001 WOODLANDS CONFERENCE AND MITCHELL PRIZE COMPETITION
Corporate Incentives and Environmental Decision Making, edited by Marilu Hastings. The Woodlands, Tex.: Center for Global Studies, Houston Advanced Research Center, 1999. The case studies prepared for the conference are available at http://files.harc.edu/Projects/Archive/Reports/EnvironmentalDecisionMaking.pdf.

Books and Reports

State Water Policies: A Study of Six States, edited by J. Schmandt, E. T. Smerdon, and J. Clarkson. New York: Praeger, 1988.

Acid Rain and Friendly Neighbors: The Policy Dispute between Canada and the United States, 2nd edition, edited by J. Schmandt, J. Clarkson, and H. Roderick. Chapel Hill, N.C.: Duke University Press, 1988.

Growth Policy in the Age of High Technology: The Role of Regions and States, edited by J. Schmandt, and R. Wilson. London: Unwin-Hyman, 1989.

Texas and Global Warming: Water Supply and Demand in Four Hydrological Regions. J. Schmandt and G. Ward, project directors. Austin: LBJ School of Public Affairs, University of Texas, 1991.

Texas and Global Warming: Emissions, Surface Water Supplies and Sea Level Rise. J. Schmandt, S. Hadden, and G. Ward, project directors. Austin: LBJ School of Public Affairs, University of Texas, 1992.

Water and Development in the Lower Rio Grande Valley. J. Schmandt and X. Mu, project directors. Austin: LBJ School of Public Affairs, University of Texas, 1992.

Water and Development in the Rio Grande/Río Bravo Basin. J. Schmandt and G. Ward, project directors. Austin: LBJ School of Public Affairs, University of Texas, 1993.

Policy Option: Responding to Climate Change in Texas. The Woodlands, Tex.: Center for Global Studies, Houston Advanced Research Center, in cooperation with the U.S. Environmental Protection Agency and the Texas Water Commission, 1993. Available at http://files.harc.edu/Projects/Archive/Reports/TexasClimateChangePolicyOptions.pdf.

Managing Environmental Risks in Texas. J. Schmandt and S. Hadden, project directors. Austin: LBJ School of Public Affairs, University of Texas, 1994.

Water and Development in Semiarid Regions — Northeast Brazil and the Rio Grande Basin. J. Schmandt, R. Wilson, and G. Ward, project directors, Austin: LBJ School of Public Affairs, University of Texas, 1995.

The Impact of Global Warming on Texas, edited by G. North, J. Schmandt, and
J. Clarkson. Austin: University of Texas Press, 1995.

Scarce Waters: Doing More with Less in the Lower Rio Grande Basin.
J. Schmandt, C. Stolp and G. Ward, project directors. Austin: U.S.-
Mexican Policy Studies Program, University of Texas, 1998.

Seeking Environmental Improvement, edited by David Hitchcock. The Woodlands, Tex.: Center for Global Studies, Houston Advanced Research Center,
1996. Report on Phase I of Houston Environmental Foresight. Available at
http://mitchell.harc.edu/Projects/Archive/Foresight/.

*The Road to Sustainable Development: A Guide for Nongovernmental Organiza-
tions.* A. Magalhães and J. Schmandt, project directors. Austin: LBJ School of
Public Affairs, University of Texas, 1998.

Sustainable Corporations: Reconciling Wealth Creation with Global Sustainability,
edited by Sunil Tankha, [1998]. Available at http://files.harc.edu/Projects/
Archive/Reports/SustainableCorporations.pdf.

*Relocation and Resettlement in Ceará: Final Report on Findings and Recommen-
dations to the Secretariat of Water Resources, State of Ceará [Brazil]*, edited by
Sunil Tankha. Available at http://files.harc.edu/Projects/Archive/Reports/
RelocationResettlementCeara.pdf.

Navigating the Waters of the Paso del Norte: A People's Guide. J. Schmandt,
C. Stolp, G. Ward, and L. Rhodes, project directors. Austin: LBJ School of
Public Affairs, University of Texas, 1999.

*Houston Cool and Green! Report of a Workshop on Climate Variability in the Hous-
ton Region*, edited by David Hitchcock. 1999. Available at http://files.harc
.edu/Projects/Archive/Reports/HoustonCoolAndGreen.pdf.

Guide to Electric Power in Texas, 3rd edition, edited by David Hitchcock.
2003. Available at http://files.harc.edu/Projects/Archive/Reports/
TexasElectricPowerGuide2003.pdf.

Houston Corridor Guide to Sustainable Development, edited by David Hitchcock. Available at http://files.harc.edu/Projects/Archive/Reports/SustainableDevelopmentGuide.pdf.

Recommendations for Environmental Improvement: Report of Houston Environmental Foresight Air Quality Work Group, January 2000, edited by David Hitchcock. Available at http://files.harc.edu/Projects/Archive/Foresight/OutdoorAndIndoorAir.pdf.

Recommendations for Environmental Improvement: Report of Houston Environmental Foresight Habitat, Parks and Water Issues Work Group, January 2000, edited by David Hitchcock. Available at http://files.harc.edu/Projects/Archive/Foresight/HabitatParksAndWater.pdf.

Recommendations for Environmental Improvement: Report of Houston Environmental Toxins and Contaminants Work Group, March 2000, edited by David Hitchcock. Available at http://files.harc.edu/Projects/Archive/Foresight/ToxinsDraft.pdf.

Water and Sustainable Development in the Binational Lower Rio Grande/Rio Bravo Basin, Final Report to the U.S. Environmental Protection Agency, 2000, edited by Mitch Mathis and Jurgen Schmandt, 2000. Available at http://mitchell.harc.edu/Archive/RioGrandeBravo/Report.

Water Planning in the Paso del Norte: Toward Regional Coordination, El Paso: Paso del Norte Water Task Force, 2001.

APPENDIX 4

Statement of the 1997 Woodlands Conference

Managing the Transition to Sustainability

Over the next few decades most demographers project a rise in world population from the current 5.7 billion to between 8 and 12 billion, following which population pressures will first stabilize, then decline. It is this transition period to sustainability—the next fifty years or so—that will require urgent and dramatic changes. We ask: *What will it take to feed, house, and employ a world population almost twice as large as today?*

The single most demanding challenge of sustainable development during this period will be to provide for the basic material and spiritual needs of this doubled world population. As the world produces and consumes more to accommodate increased needs, additional stress will be exerted on existing natural, social, and economic systems. Sustainable development demands that we not only meet these needs but that we do so in a manner which will not irreparably damage the more crowded life-support systems of our planet.

How can this be done? First of all, the transition period must find better ways for reconciling market-based economic growth and development on the one hand, and alleviation of poverty and greater equity on the other. Secondly, sustainable development challenges our existing mental maps, requiring new ways of thinking that rely less on "invisible hands" and more on the proactive and integrated actions of an educated citizenry and leadership. Thirdly, dealing proactively with the transition requires that we realize that our scientific knowledge and understanding of the intricacies of the complex and intertwined life-support systems of this planet are still rudimentary. We cannot, and should not, wait for full information about these systems to be available before deciding upon action. Fourthly, we must acknowledge the power of market-based systems in generating income and furthering development. This means that policies for environmental protection, poverty alleviation, and community development should be crafted to complement market forces, not work against them. Finally, stakeholder participation in decision making and dispute resolution is the key to eradicating the poverty and unequal distribution of resources and wealth that disfigure our world.

Vision

Vision is the cohesive force in the quest for sustainability. While a myriad of discrete individual actions will determine our future, a common vision must drive and direct these actions. Our first step toward sustainability must be to collectively decide on where we want to go. Continuing ambiguity on what constitutes sustainable development only opens up opportunities for disguising various agendas under the cloak of sustainability.

Our vision of sustainability in the twenty-first century is a world free, first of all, of extreme poverty and social as well as political inequality. Having evoked our responsibility to future, yet unborn generations, sustainable development discourses have somewhat shifted our focus away from spatial inequality and poverty reduction efforts in the present and toward temporal equality and environmental protection for the future. In reality, these issues are two sides of the same coin. It is well documented that poverty and environmental degradation and high birth rates are coincident. Reiterating Indian prime minister Indira Gandhi's declaration before the 1972 Stockholm Summit on the Human Environment that "poverty is the greatest polluter," we call for the adoption of poverty alleviation as the first order of business in the transition period.

We envision a sustainable world that has found the appropriate balance between human activity and the ability of the ecosystems—at the local, regional, and global levels—to accommodate these activities without the loss of long-term carrying capacity. Such a balance will enable us to mitigate the threat of global warming and other environmental problems that endanger life on this planet. Achieving this balance rests upon our accepting the fact that there are certain incontrovertible limits to the absorptive capacity of the biosphere. We do not yet know where these limits lie, but we do know that they exist.

Personal and institutional responsibility for actions that promote sustainability is at the heart of successfully managing the transition. A sustainable world, we believe, is equally dependent upon institutions capable of motivating human behavior and the economy consistent with the principles of sustainable use of earth's resources. Such institutions include a private sector that is fully committed to making practical contributions to sustainability; a public sector that accepts its obligation to set common ground rules for sustainability, and a third, nongovernmental and community sector that addresses the more personal, philosophical, and spiritual aspects of sustainability.

We realize that this vision of a sustainable world can only be achieved gradually. But we also state categorically that the time for action is now. We must start incorporating the necessary transformations in our economic, sociocultural, and political systems. Otherwise it may be too late.

Challenges

Adapting to the new conditions that govern the survival of our society and our planet and its life-support systems is the most compelling challenge in our history. Our success or failure in meeting this endeavor will have repercussions not only for future generations but for all life on earth. Answering this challenge will require us to remold current modes of social, economic, and political behavior into models more compatible with sustainable development. Specifically, we must commit to three discrete though interlinked changes: changing current paths, changing mindsets and behavior, and changing consumption patterns.

Changing Current Paths

As we enter the twenty-first century, we face several crises that must be addressed in the transition to sustainable development. These include population growth, increasing poverty and inequality, global climate change, inadequate supplies of food and clean water, dependence upon polluting and nonrenewable sources of energy, and local and regional conflict.

In many cases, the scientific and technological knowledge exists to resolve or at least mitigate these problems. What is lacking is the political and moral will to ask the necessary but difficult and often controversial questions: Is it rational to assume a growth component in national economies that increases exponentially forever? Who decides which resources are to be used and by whom? Can every culture become sustainable? How dependent is manufactured capital and income on natural capital?

We can avoid unsustainable paths by addressing the basic flaws in our current systems and rejecting the stock answers we have relied on in the past that cannot be expected to solve the problems we face today.

Education that stresses the principles of and approaches to sustainability is the key in this effort. The biggest barrier to this is existing educational structures that do not recognize the importance of sustainability and remain wedded to old paradigms of teaching. We must encourage schools, colleges, and universities to develop sustainable development curricula and encourage interdisciplinary approaches to the investigation of environmental and social crises.

Changing Mental Maps and Behavior
A change in our sociocultural, economic, and political thinking is predicated upon changing the mental maps we work with. These maps were etched into our consciousness when the earth was relatively empty of humans and bereft of human impact. They were drawn to act within cultures of consumption. They also resorted frequently to conflict for resolving differences between nations and ethnic groups.

For example, even today, after so much has been written on the need to cooperate for sustainability, much of our social and economic system remains mired in the need to compete. Our concepts of economic development are still based upon quantitative increases in gross national product. Our concept of welfare is still measured in terms of consumption. Many still put forward the "jobs versus environment" argument.

Changing mental maps is a very slow process. We stress here that the processes of redesigning our mental circuitry requires integrated approaches from a wide variety of perspectives. Progress depends upon education and spiritual reawakening. In our view, changing mental maps and behavior is absolutely essential in managing the transition period. To date, this side of sustainable development has not received the attention it deserves.

Changing Consumption Patterns
Growth in population and consumption is at the heart of environmental and social stresses. We know much about the former, not enough about the latter. Giving current conditions, less than a 10 percent increase in the population in the developed world will have as much of an ecological impact as a doubling

of population in the developing world. This highlights the need for paying much closer attention to consumption. Patterns of consumption and lifestyles in the developed world may already be unsustainable. Yet these same patterns and lifestyles are pursued by the populations of developing nations that legitimately strive for economic development. We know that the world does not have enough resources available to bring these consumption patterns to everyone on earth.

Changing consumption patterns is essential so that future generations of today's poor may become better off, so that unsustainability may not be transmitted from the first world to the third world through trade and globalization, and so that humans may not destroy the ecological space of other living organisms. As we make the required changes in consumption patterns we will automatically change the character of economic growth and of development.

How do we change consumption patterns? A first step is to realize that a better quality of life is linked to a better environment. That is, it is not necessarily a question of consuming less, but a question of substituting one (environmentally harmful) pleasure for another (environmentally benign) pleasure.

On the supply side of this issue the starting point is well understood, though not equally well practiced: reduce, reuse, recycle—the 3 R's. But on the demand side there is no popular consensus. The preference seems to be the slogan "Everybody change but us."

Changing consumption patterns may harm, in the short term, some sectors of the economy and the workforce. That is why we have protest whenever we put restrictions on human activity that harms the environment. But this pain is transient, quickly soothed by other emerging occupational opportunities.

The best form of advocacy for managing the transition to a sustainable world lies in presenting an alternative vision. This vision of change consists of two separate elements: the first is the development of a strategic approach to sustainability and the second is the construction of practical steps that execute the strategy. In the preceding sections we have attempted to outline the vision; we now shift our focus to implementation.

Ethics and Leadership

Spirituality and sustainable development. It is difficult to picture change at the scale necessary to create sustainable societies without mobilizing human spirituality. Ethics and leadership are the foundations for managing the transition to sustainable development. They will dictate the manner in which we will respond to the challenge. They will make possible the many detailed changes that are needed in technology and policy. Conversely, without ethical change, managing the transition is likely to fail.

The ethics of the future must include a reverence for the earth and for the maintenance of the earth as a functioning environmental system. This spiritual relationship will include a sense of place and a sense of connection with the ecological systems that span national and international boundaries and interests. It is consistent with organized religious views as well as secular views of environmental philosophy and needs to become part of our daily lives.

Changing ethics, however, is not an easy task. To realize these changes, as much use as possible should be made of existing institutions. As traditional centers for empowerment and spiritual and moral transformation, religious organizations are well positioned to lead the reformation of the world view vis-à-vis the natural world. Having already focused on poverty and education, religious organizations must again focus on changing worldviews from an orientation toward conflict and profit to interdependence and reverence. To further these goals they must promote the organization, formation, and sustenance of local communities of support, inspiration, and activism.

After a considerable period of ignoring the spiritual side of nature, serious reflection and reconsideration undertaken by Judeo-Christian scholars is culminating in a revision of earth-related theology. This incorporation of spiritual connections to the natural world into organized church activity can greatly aid in bringing about the required changes in our mental maps. Valuable lessons are also to be learned from the many indigenous cultures and religions whose ethical foundations in nature-based value systems offer examples of life-sustaining beliefs: a spiritual regard for the environment, a devotion to future generations, and commitment to community life.

Leadership for sustainable development. In the absence of concrete evidence to the contrary, the rhetoric surrounding sustainable development often divides itself into discrete, incompatible camps. It is at this juncture that leadership plays the critical role. Sustainable development must not be allowed to become the domain of any one ideology or political philosophy. Its appeal must extend beyond such territorial claims. It must be made to appeal as much to the loggers and the fishermen as to environmentalists. It is therefore critical that our leaders who articulate this new vision do not cling defensively to old constituencies. This would guarantee only transient change dictated by which ideology currently holds sway in the halls of government.

Leadership needed to manage the transition is democratic, consultative, and literate in natural and social sciences. How can we get such leadership? First, a concentrated effort must be made to educate our legislators and representatives on sustainable development issues.

But education alone is the solution only as far as ignorance is the problem. Our systems of governance must be suffused with a strong environmental ethic that guides action. Leadership for sustainable development must become associated with nurture and cooperation rather than domination. It must also address difficult choices to be made in the distribution of economic goods through the marketplace. As citizens, we must support these activities by allowing our elected representatives the latitude to learn through trial and error as they search for difficult answers to pressing problems.

The Scientific Community and Decision Making under Uncertainty

Human actions are, to a greater or lesser extent, conditioned and constrained by our understanding (or lack thereof) of how the natural world works. Thus, science has the potential to play a critical role in informing decision makers of the impacts of human activities on the behavior of the earth's ecosystems. To realize this potential fully, science must confront several challenges and tensions:

1. *Reconciling the need for research "unfettered" by specific mission or need and research prioritized by compelling needs or applications.* Competing interests for scarce resources makes it imperative that we strike the right balance between research that expands the outer boundaries of our scientific knowledge base and research that may be less glamorous but nonetheless is central to sound decision making regarding the future. Certain kinds of data and knowledge deserve higher priorities precisely because they are critical to our survival.
2. *Developing systems-level scientific inquiries that combine natural and social sciences.* While reductionist approaches are often critical to understanding nature, synthetic, systems-level assessments and collaborations are

necessary to understand the behavior of complex systems. Integrated assessments offer a promising avenue of bringing together various competing and complementing forces. Many of the environmental impacts are created by nonenvironmental policies and development projects. By viewing these issues clinically in isolation for the sake of pure science robs us of a better understanding of the impact of our actions.

3. *Increasing the level of communication between the scientific community and stakeholders and decision makers.* Public understanding of the concerns discovered by the scientific community is critical. Scientists must communicate not just knowledge but also an understanding of and confidence in how that knowledge was acquired. Citizens for their part should not expect complete information, but they must be assured that information is presented in good faith. Science can "tell us what will happen," "tell us the probability of its happening," and "tell us how we know." Citizens will choose to use this information in the context of social, cultural, economic, and political knowledge or values.

As an agent of change in the transition to sustainability, science and the management and policy on which it is based must be adaptive to

1. *Unique conditions and cultures.* Appropriate technologies are required as "one size fits all" approaches are unlikely to deliver required benefits.
2. *A changing world.* It is at least as important to appreciate the fact of change as its direction. Questions related to the conservation of biodiversity, for example, often deconstruct to "how many do we need?" or "how few can we get by with?" not recognizing that those questions only have meaning when we also ask "for how long?" or "what if the world changes?" Also, increased population growth will continue to push humans into marginal environments—which is just where suffering is greatest when the world changes.
3. *New knowledge and understanding.* Scientific understanding is provisional. We must shorten the lag time between the acquisition of knowledge and its application to real world challenges.

Adaptive management requires clear goals and objectives informed by a shared mental model. Examples of this include agreement on the inviolability of the laws of thermodynamics, principles of human equity and justice, and the sanctity of life. It also requires monitoring systems that include indicators and benchmarks informed by our best understanding of how the world works. These should include descriptive indicators such as report cards and diagnostic indicators such as CAT scans. Such systems must provide timely feedback of information.

Decision making in the context of uncertainty: We never do what *is* right, only what we *think* is right. Accepting that our knowledge is limited and provisional, and that there may be limits to what we can know and predict, we must also accept the need to act on the knowledge and understanding in our possession. Action is urgent. Uncertainty must not stand in the way. Inaction is not "neutral ground" to which we can retreat in the face of uncertainty. Doing nothing has its own consequences and opportunity costs.

Tools for Managing the Transition

The private sector has a central role to play in the transition to sustainable development. Corporations alone are in a position to access, domestically and on a global scale, the resources and technologies required to make the transition to sustainability possible.

Industrial ecology is one attempt to begin to establish the scientific and technological base for progress toward an environmentally and economically efficient, sustainable global economy. Its primary goal is to achieve a state of sustainable material use as a part of a sustainable economy. However, more time must be spent in boardrooms evaluating the sustainability of the corporations.

Environmental and resource issues at corporations should be treated not as overhead but as strategic considerations. As yet, environmental policies are generally taken into account only after the main decisions regarding production and marketing have been made. The new approach of integrating them into mainstream activities from the beginning is to be encouraged. This change of perspective makes it possible for businesses to exploit sustainable development practices as marketing tools to retain and gain customers and as a means to enhance shareholder values.

While corporate behavior must change to embrace new technologies and new products that are more efficient in terms of material and energy content, corporations will continue to take their cues from the market. How success-fully the capitalist market economy is able to incorporate the demands of the environment and society will therefore be a key determinant of our ability to achieve sustainability.

The market must evolve suitably to reward corporations that take seri-ously their environmental responsibilities, and punish those that do not. Ap-propriate signals must be given—through social norms and political rules—that indicate to business leaders the effectiveness of sustainable development policies.

Command and control regulations have, in many places, outlived their use-fulness. Such regulations were necessary to implement the first tier of change from an unbounded economic system. Their successes have, however, come at the cost of increased bureaucracy, and hence, decreased efficiency. Com-mand and control mechanisms are also vulnerable to changing political prior-ities, thus inhibiting long-term strategic planning. Innovative approaches and market-system concepts can and should be used to encourage movement into the next tier of change. A first step is to reevaluate inefficient tax and subsidy policies that encourage patterns of economic activity that do not minimize the flow of materials and energy into and out of the economic system.

Many corporations have already taken the lead in demonstrating environ-mental responsibility, and have shown that given flexibility, they can combine profitability, efficiency, and environmental stewardship. But because of the heavy reliance on regulations, much of corporate energy remains focused on pollution control and regulatory compliance. When governments mandate processes and procedures, the only incentive they create is for firms to do the bare minimum that is required by law. This is inefficient and passes on extra costs to consumers. Regulation should be instituted by goals instead of methods. This would enable corporations to minimize the cost of achieving sustainability by allowing them to do what they do best, that is, figure out the best technical solutions to policy goals.

The capitalist market system offers a basis for transaction and a framework of incentives. Well-designed market tools for sustainability contain within them a better and more efficient means of providing the information that pro-ducers, consumers, and decision makers require in order to make sound judg-ments for the sustainable future of our planet. Performance standards such as the ISO 14000 are able to provide this information in an efficient manner.

Tools such as full-cost accounting and life-cycle analysis can further promote sustainable practices by bringing to the forefront all the environmental costs associated with the production, distribution, and consumption of a product or service. Cost shifting tendencies should be reduced and prices should reflect marginal social costs, thereby providing appropriate and correct signals to decision makers in the economic and political process.

A concern raised repeatedly at the conference was whether a global economy and environmental protection could go hand-in-hand. Unguided market forces will not move the economy toward sustainability. Sustainable development requires the innovative stimulus of the free-market economy but without its indifference to income concentration and unemployment.

Government needs to provide the leadership to ensure that market mechanisms promote environmental and social concerns in an efficient manner and provide adequate distribution of essential commodities to all. However, certain objectives can only be achieved by public action, often on an international scale. It is the global community's responsibility to remain vigilant against practices that will endanger the long-term viability of our society.

Stakeholders and Dispute Resolution

Development over the last few decades has led to dramatic improvements in living conditions in some countries, and considerable social and economic dislocation in other places. Historically, the poor and marginalized sections of society have been denied a say in decisions that directly and indirectly affect their futures. Consequently, they have also been denied an equitable share in the distribution of resources and gains from economic activity.

The social dimension of sustainable development requires that local people take a leading position in development initiatives. As it is the poor and marginalized sector of the world population that will rapidly double over the next few decades, it is important that a capability of collective action be established in these communities in order for them to secure the political and economic rights and privileges to which they are entitled.

Stakeholder approaches to development decision making, stressing the participation of representatives of all affected interests, are new and dynamic initiatives that have the potential to achieve the type of integrated problem solving that will be needed to reach a more sustainable future. Such participatory decision making establishes a sense of ownership of all interested parties in regard to a specific action, be it a program, a project, or a legal act. It provides for consensus building, and hence, political sustainability of decisions that affect the lives and interests of different people and entities.

Stakeholder participation extends beyond mere outreach. It must be responsive to the diversity of interests that will be affected by the outcome of policy decisions. It therefore requires the genuine participation of all interested parties in the decision-making processes that affect them. If stakeholder processes do not include representatives of all interests, they only reinforce existing weaknesses of the disempowered groups. Hence stakeholder participation is an organized process that may assume different forms according to the specifics of the action or of the participants.

In order to assure a fair process of participation, a first step is the identification of all relevant stakeholders. It is the responsibility of the private sector not only to allow for stakeholder participation—in and outside of the company—but also to participate in other social and government decisions where the participating stakeholders may have a role.

Dispute resolution between competing stakeholders, business, and government is critical to sustainability. Conflict is costly and inefficient. Effective dispute resolution, however, requires that the playing field first be leveled through the empowerment of local populations. Empowerment is education of the legal and economic rights and the realization of social power.

It is always possible to overcome conflict through direct negotiations or the mediation of commonly agreed upon mechanisms, according to rules previously accepted. In many ways, a proper process of stakeholder participation is enough to deal with, and to overcome potential and actual conflict.

There exists presently a number of techniques and methodologies in regard to stakeholder participation and conflict resolution. Arbitration and mediation are two concepts that have worked to achieve significant reductions in emissions and improvement in the performance of major industries. Integrated regional assessments, involving dialogues between experts and stakeholders, have shown promise in regional sustainability planning. Such techniques and methodologies should be disseminated. Wider use of these concepts on a voluntary basis could significantly improve the relations between government, industry, and community.

Willingness to work with affected parties to resolve disputes is not a sign of weakness. Instead, it is the type of behavior that typifies the requirement for cooperative action to substitute for patterns of domination that have prevailed in decision-making processes to date.

Bringing It Together

Before we can change, certain difficult technical questions have to be addressed and resolved. For example, how much growth can we enjoy, and of what kind, before it becomes environmentally harmful? How can we control population and consumption? How will the increased human presence affect other living creatures? How can we ensure welfare for all citizens under the new growth structures? These are a sample of the questions that were regularly asked by conference attendees. To these concerns, we currently have no definitive answers. The critical challenge that this poses is, given this uncertainty, can we move forward or will we be trapped in endless debate?

We do not advocate a full-blown blueprint for change that will outline in detailed steps all that needs to be done to ensure a sustainable earth. The process of discovering these individual steps cannot be coordinated into a well-packaged whole. It is inherently an incremental process and we learn step-by-step by doing. The urgency that we stress is in getting started on the road to sustainable development.

We feel optimistic about the future. Human creativity thrives on challenge, and we are confident that a solution will be found. But it will require going beyond ethical changes, beyond voluntary measures, and beyond technical fixes, to the creation of a shared vision of a sustainable and desirable society. With a common language on sustainability we can develop a broad understanding so that individual action is part of a synergistic and comprehensive approach to sustainability that leverages all sectors of society.

APPENDIX 5

Club of Rome Lifetime Achievement Award for George and Cynthia Mitchell

Aurelio Peccei predicted critical elements to solving the earth's pressing problems of lack of a sustainable pattern of development and future. Aurelio Peccei was known to all of us as a visionary, a global thinker, a brilliant generalist, and our leader and founder because he made us go beyond ourselves, but he was a practical-minded businessman, coming from the automotive industry. He was well-seasoned by the world of reality.

He would have been happy to be here today to award this medal (named in his honor) to George and Cynthia Mitchell. This husband-and-wife team of effective visionary thinkers as well as "doers" have embodied within their life's work the principles and philosophy that Aurelio taught the world.

The Peccei Principles embodied in the lives of the George and Cynthia Mitchell team have occurred in several phases. The vision of the future and the intuition to move forward on this vision was seen in George Mitchell's early achievements in the gas and oil business. He recognized the importance of producing a more environmentally friendly energy source (natural gas), and he created the technological skills to add substantial amounts of environmental safeguards to the extraction and transshipment of the natural gas. The advances in the United States' use of gas rather than oil are of known importance globally.

George and Cynthia Mitchell were able to listen and hear what others like Aurelio Peccei, Buckminster Fuller, and Harland Cleveland were envisioning. Through their unique transcultural method, they brought critical parts of the industrial and financial community to focus on the capacity to recognize these visions, particularly the concept of sustainability for human and environmental needs. They did this through several venues directly conceived and executed by the Mitchells. A few of the Mitchells' highlights are:

1. The Mitchells' Conferences on Sustainability opened the concepts of critical need for sustainability of resources and environmental accounting of degradation by bringing together leaders from both the industrial/financial world and Peccei's world of sustainable global thinking to debate and educate one another about these issues.

2. The Houston Advanced Research Center (HARC) with its Center for Global Studies sponsored conferences on problems of sustainability and brought together many Texas universities with their intellectual talent to this subject.

3. The Mitchells had a vision of sustainable communities and an ability to recognize cultural change and were able to carry this out within the present system. This created an important addition to Texas real estate development in the 1960s (when "green" in real estate meant a golf course). The Mitchells' development concept of "The Woodlands"—a community featuring sustainable energy sources, nature among dwellings and businesses, and bike paths for local transport—introduced to Texas an array of sustainable living techniques in a superb setting, leading the way to sustainability in real estate development in Texas. It also was the top leader in new home sales in Texas for seven straight years.

4. In the philanthropic work of George and Cynthia Mitchell, they foresaw the future and recognized that their concept of the future could be used for the common good for a wide variety of peoples. They acted locally, but transculturally, as their genius produced important results over a range of disciplines and institutions, adding up to a more sustainable world for the future. Notable among these are the following:

1. Restoration of cultural and social values in historically important Texas communities such as Galveston, where both historic building restoration along "the Strand" as well as the historic revivals of festivals such as Mardi Gras, were directly begun by the Mitchells;

2. Grants for researching medical solutions for critical medical problems determining life quality in the future such as Alzheimer's disease, cancer, and optical disorders;

3. Contributions to critical scientific work such as in astronomy, engineering, marine science, biophysical medical optics, and fundamental physics at the University of Texas and Texas A&M University;

4. Creation of charter schools for the University of Texas; and

5. The endowment to the National Academy of Sciences that created the Sustainable Futures programs, which has turned the focus of some of the most effective minds in the United States toward the problems of future sustainability.

The particular actions of Cynthia Mitchell in establishing the Global Children's Foundation, which provides safe havens for young victims of war and tyranny, the Cynthia Mitchell Chair of Theater at the University of Houston and her distinguished authors series, and her work with the Houston Youth Symphony and Ballet and the Texas Music Festival deserves comment as part of her vision of the future, especially for children.

The husband-and-wife team of George and Cynthia Mitchell have demonstrated over their lifetimes a quest for a global vision of a world sustaining itself. This quest has resulted in innumerable important actions that have created a more sustainable world.

NOTES

Introduction

1. Garrett Hardin, "The Tragedy of the Commons," *Science* 162 (1968): 1243–48. Some historians have taken issue with the accuracy of Hardin's reading of the historical record, but their critique does not invalidate his analysis of the social dynamic at work. For a recent review of the commons problem see National Research Council, *The Drama of the Commons* (Washington, D.C.: National Academy Press, 2002).

2. Jared Diamond, *Collapse: How Societies Choose to Fail or Succeed* (New York: Viking, 2003).

3. Jeffrey Sachs, "The New Geopolitics," *Scientific American*, June 2006, 30.

Chapter 1. George P. Mitchell

1. Sheila McNulty, "The Last of the Wildcatters," *Financial Times*, February 22, 2008, 48, http://www.ft.com/cms/s/2/f63ced54-de91-11dc-9de3-0000779fd2ac.html (accessed September 22, 2009). For a contemporary account of how the Mitchell brothers got started on their North Texas field see "Oil & Gas: A Word to the Wise," *Time Magazine*, December 17, 1956, http://www.time.com/time/magazine/article/0,9171,867456,00.html (accessed September 22, 2009).

2. "Potential Gas Committee Reports Unprecedented Increase in Mag-nitude of U.S. Natural Gas Resource Base," news release, June 18, 2009, Colorado School of Mines, http://www.mines.edu/Potential-Gas-Committee-reports-unprecedented-increase-in-magnitude-of-U.S.-natural-gas-resource-base (accessed July 17, 2009). The report itself: Potential Gas Committee, *Potential Supply of Natural Gas in the United States (December 31, 2008)* (Golden, Colo.: Colorado School of Mines, 2008).

3. Rick Smead and Gordon Pickering, "An Unconventional Future," *World Gas* 3.2 (2009): 124–28, http://uk.reuters.com/article/idUKN3048271520080730?pageNumber=2&virtualBrandChannel=0&sp=true (accessed July 17, 2009).

4. Geoffrey Styles, "Shale Gas and Climate Change," Energy Outlook, posted June 5, 2009, http://energyoutlook.blogspot.com/2009/06/shale-gas-and-climate-change.html (accessed August 2009).

5. J. Bogan, "The Father of Shale Gas," Forbes.com, July 16, 2009, http://www.forbes.com/2009/07/16/george-mitchell-gas-business-energy-shale.html. (accessed August 2009).

6. Todd Mitchell, personal conversation with George Mitchell, April 6, 2006.

7. Michel Halbouty, quoted in Joseph W. Kutchin, *How Mitchell Energy and Development Corp. Got Its Start and*

How It Grew (updated) [The Woodlands, Tex.]: Universal Publishers, 2001), 468.

8. George P. Mitchell, interview with Lawrence Goodwin and Barbara Griffith, April 16, 1993, reprinted in Kutchin, *How Mitchell Energy and Development Corp. Got Its Start*, 445.

9. Shaker A. Khayatt, quoted in Kutchin, *How Mitchell Energy and Development Corp. Got Its Start*, 278.

10. Kutchin, *How Mitchell Energy and Development Corp. Got Its Start.* A brief account of the ups and downs of the company is available at http://www.fundinguniverse.com/company-histories/Mitchell-Energy-and-Development-Corporation-Company-History.html (accessed December 2, 2007).

11. George P. Mitchell, interview by Jurgen Schmandt, February 9, 2006.

12. Mitchell interview, February 9, 2006.

13. Cabell Brand, interview by Jurgen Schmandt, March 27, 2007.

14. Robert Hartsfield, quoted in Kutchin, *How Mitchell Energy and Development Corp. Got Its Start*, 247.

15. Ian McHarg, *Design with Nature* (Garden City, N.Y.: Natural History Press, 1969).

16. Hartsfield, quoted in Kutchin, *How Mitchell Energy and Development Corp. Got Its Start*, 238.

17. Wikipedia contributors, "Ian McHarg," *Wikipedia, the Free Encyclopedia*, http://en.wikipedia.org/w/index.php?title=Ian_McHarg&oldid=337864044 (accessed February 13, 2010).

18. Erik Slotboom, *Houston Freeways: A Historical and Visual Journey* (Houston: O. F. Slotboom, 2003), 48.

19. George T. Morgan Jr. and John O.

King, *The Woodlands: New Community Development, 1964–1983* (College Station: Texas A&M University Press).

20. Ruthanne Haut, *Environmental Action Plan: The Woodlands, TX*, December 15, 2006, p. 8, http://files.harc.edu/Documents/Announcements/2007/WoodandsEnvironmentalActionPlan.pdf (accessed October 9, 2009).

21. Mitchell interview, February 9, 2006.

22. E. F. Schumacher, *Small Is Beautiful: Economics as if People Mattered* (London: Blond and Briggs, 1973).

Chapter 2. The History of Sustainability

1. Ulrich Grober, "Der Erfinder der Nachhaltigkeit," in *Die Zeit*, Nr. 48, November 25, 1999, 98. See also Grober's articles, "Die Idee der Nachhaltigkeit als zivilisatorischer Entwurf" [The Concept of Sustainability as a Draft for Civilization], in *Aus Politik und Zeitgeschichte* 24 (2001): 5, and "Modewort mit tiefen Wurzeln—Kleine Begriffsgeschichte von 'sustainability' und 'Nachhaltigkeit,'" in *Jahrbuch Ökologie 2003* (München: Beck, 2002), 167–75.

2. Hans Carl von Carlowitz, *Sylvicultura Oeconomica* (Leipzig: Johann Friedrich Braun, 1713), 105–6.

3. A standard work on the history of forestry acknowledges the significance of *Sylvicultura Oeconomica* for scientific forestry but makes no reference to its recommendations for sustainable harvests. See Bernhard Eduard Fernow, *A Brief History of Forestry in Europe, the United States and other Countries* (Toronto: University Press, 1907), 80. The same is true of a more recent study, N. D. G. James, "A History of Forestry and Monographic Forestry Literature in Germany,

France, and the United Kingdom," in *The Literature of Forestry and Agroforestry*, ed. Peter McDonald and James Lassoie (Ithaca, N.Y.: Cornell University, 1966), 15–44. To the same volume, James Coufal and Donald Webster contributed a paper, "The Emergence of Sustainable Forestry," which moves directly from the Bible to American forestry in the nineteenth and twentieth centuries.

4. Georg Ludwig Hartig, introduction to *Anweisung zur Taxation und Beschreibung der Forste*, 2nd ed. (Wiesbaden 1804), http://books.google.de (accessed July 18, 2009).

5. Ernst Haeckel, *General Morphology of Organisms; General Outlines of the Science of Organic Forms Based on Mechanical Principles through the Theory of Descent as Reformed by Charles Darwin* (Berlin, 1866).

6. See Pascal Acot, Patrick Blandin, and Jean-Marc Drouin, *The European Origins of Scientific Ecology* (New York: Routledge, 1998).

7. Quoted in W. C. Adams, *The Future of Sustainability, Rethinking Environment and Development in the Twenty-first Century*, Report of the IUCN (World Conservation Union) Renowned Thinkers Meeting, January 29–31, 2006, http://www.iucn.org/ (accessed October 10, 2006).

8. IUCN, *The World Conservation Strategy: Living Resource Conservation for Sustainable Development* (Geneva: International Union for Conservation of Nature and Natural Resources, United Nations Environment Programme, World Wildlife Fund, 1980). WWF is now the Worldwide Fund for Nature. IUCN is now the World Conservation Union.

9. World Commission on Environment and Development, *Our Common*

Future (Oxford: Oxford University Press, 1987).

10. United Nations, General Assembly, *2005 World Summit Outcome*, September 15, 2005, p. 12.

11. WCED, *Our Common Future*, 49.

12. United Nations, *Agenda 21 Earth Summit: Program of Action from Rio* (New York: United Nations, 1992).

13. George P. Mitchell, interview by Jurgen Schmandt, April 18, 2006.

Chapter 3. The Need for Sustainable Development

1. E. Deevey, "The Human Population," *Scientific American*, September 1960, 194–204.

2. Paul R. Ehrlich and Anne H. Ehrlich, *Population-Resources-Environment: Issues in Human Ecology* (San Francisco: W. H. Freeman, 1970), 1.

3. Joel E. Cohen, "Human Population Grows Up," *Scientific American*, September 2005, 48–55.

4. Peter M. Vitousek, Harold A. Mooney, Jane Lubchenco, and Jerry M. Melillo, "Human Domination of Earth's Ecosystems," *Science* 277 (July 25, 1997): 494, 498.

5. Tikva Frymer-Kensky, "The Atrahasis Epic and Its Significance for our Understanding of Genesis 1–9," *Biblical Archaeologist* 40 (1977): 147–55.

6. Thomas Malthus, preface to *An Essay on the Principle of Population* (London, 1798).

7. Lester Brown, *Seeds of Change* (New York: Praeger, 1970).

8. Environmental scientists generally agree that growth in population, in wealth, and in technology cause environmental problems.

9. The following sections on successive waves of industrial revolution

are based on my article "The Future of Science and Technology in the United States," *The World & I*, November 1988, 150–61.

10. For a recent review of the subject, see Espen Moe, "The Economic Rise and Fall of the Great Powers: Technological and Industrial Leadership since the Industrial Revolution," *World Political Science Review* 3, no. 2 (2007), article 1, http://www.bepress.com/wpsr/vol3/iss2/art1/ (accessed February 14, 2010).

11. Robert C. Allen, *The British Industrial Revolution in Global Perspective* (Cambridge: Cambridge University Press, 2009).

12. The British Navy used a prototype of the assembly line, but the economic importance of this approach was not recognized in England.

Chapter 4. The Club of Rome

1. Alexander King, *Let the Cat Turn Around: One Man's Traverse of the Twentieth Century* (London: CPTM, 2006), 296.

2. Jean-Jacques Salomon, "Hommage á Alexander King," *Futuribles*, Mai 2007, 81–83.

3. Aurelio Peccei, *The Human Quality* (Oxford: Pergamon Press, 1977), 63.

4. King, *Let the Cat Turn Around*, 296.

5. King, *Let the Cat Turn Around*, 297.

6. For a detailed history of the Club of Rome see "Declaration of the Club of Rome," April 25, 1996, http://www.mega.nu/ampp/cor.html (accessed May 7, 2007).

7. Donella H. Meadows, Dennis L. Meadows, Jørgen Randers and William W. Behrens, foreword to *The Limits to Growth*, Potomac Associates edition (New York: Universe Books, 1972), 9.

8. Jay Forester, *World Dynamics* (Cambridge, Mass.: Wright-Allen, 1971).

9. Dennis Meadows, interview Jurgen Schmandt, March 14, 2007, p. 7.

10. Dennis L. Meadows, William W. Behrens III, Donella H. Meadows, Roger F. Naill, Jørgen Randers, and Erich K. O. Zahn *The Dynamics of Growth in a Finite World* (Cambridge, Mass.: Wright-Allen Press, 1974), and Dennis L. Meadows and Donella Meadows, *Toward Global Equilibrium* (Cambridge, Mass.: Wright-Allen Press, 1973).

11. Cited in Eleonara Barbieri Massini, "The Legacy of Aurelio Peccei Twenty Years after His Passing and the Continuing Relevance of His Anticipatory Vision," 2004 Aurelio Peccei Lecture, Rome, November 23, 2004, http://www.clubofrome.at/archive/mas-peccei.html (accessed February 14, 2010).

12. Caption of figure 46 in Meadows, *Limits to Growth*, 168.

13. Dennis L. Meadows, "30-Year Update of Limits to Growth Finds Global Society in 'Overshoot,' Foresees Social, Economic, and Environmental Decline," presentation to the Annual Conference of the Club of Rome, Helsinki, 2004, http://www.clubofrome.org (accessed February 14, 2010). See also Donella Meadows, Jørgen Randers, and Dennis Meadows, *Limits to Growth: The 30-Year Update* (White River Junction, Vt.: Chelsea Green Publishing Co., 2004), and Dennis Meadows, "Evaluating Past Forecasts: Reflections on One Critique of *The Limits to Growth*," in *Sustainability or Collapse?* ed. Robert Costanza, Lisa J. Graumlich, and Will Steffen (Cambridge, Mass.: MIT Press, 2007), 399–415.

14. Meadows interview, March 14, 2007, p. 15.

15. Meadows, *Limits to Growth*, 29.

16. Edward Goldsmith and Robert Allen, "A Blueprint for Survival," *The Ecologist* 2, no. 1 (January 1972), http://www.theecologist.info/page34.html (accessed February 14, 2010).

17. Charles V. Kidd, "The Evolution of Sustainability," *Journal of Agricultural and Environmental Ethics* 5, no. 1 (March 1992): 1–26.

18. *A Blueprint for Survival* (Harmondsworth: Penguin Books; Boston: Houghton Mifflin, 1972).

19. Mihajlo Mesarovic and Eduard Pestel, *Mankind at the Turning Point — The Second Report to the Club of Rome* (New York: E. P. Dutton, 1974).

20. Mesarovic and Pestel, *Mankind at the Turning Point*, ix.

21. Mesarovic and Pestel, *Mankind at the Turning Point*, 7.

22. Mesarovic and Pestel, *Mankind at the Turning Point*, 203.

Chapter 5. Early Woodlands Conferences

1. George P. Mitchell, interview by Jurgen Schmandt, March 9, 2006, p. 14.

2. Mitchell interview, March 9, 2006.

3. George Mitchell interview, May 15, 1996, in Kutchin, *How Mitchell Energy and Development Corp. Got Its Start*, 426.

4. George P. Mitchell, interview by Jurgen Schmandt, May 3, 2006.

5. Mitchell interview, March 22, 2006.

6. Mitchell interview, March 9, 2006.

7. Mitchell interview, March 22, 2006.

8. Dennis L. Meadows, *Alternatives to Growth I: The Search for Sustainable Futures* (Cambridge, Mass.: Ballinger Publishing Company, 1977), xvii.

9. Meadows, *Alternatives to Growth I*, xviii.

10. Mitchell interview, March 9, 2006.

11. Naisbitt later wrote two influential books: *Megatrends: Ten New Directions Transforming Our Lives* (New York: Warner Books, 1982) and *Reinventing the Corporation: Transforming Your Job and Your Company for the New Information Society* (New York: Warner Books, 1985).

12. The quote from Molly Ivins is reprinted in *The Woodlands Forum* (HARC Center for Global Studies) 10, no. 2 (Winter 1993–94): 8.

13. Susan Grinton Orr, ed., "An Inquiry into the Nature of Sustainable Societies: A History of the Evolution and Content of the Woodlands Conference" (Houston: The Woodlands Center for Growth Studies, no date), mimeographed manuscript, p. 6.

14. Mitchell interview, March 9, 2006.

15. Meadows interview, March 14, 2007, p. 11.

16. The paper is published in D. L. Meadows, *Alternatives to Growth I*, 135–53.

17. D. Meadows, "Equity, the Free Market, and the Sustainable State," in D. L. Meadows, *Alternatives to Growth I*, 152.

18. Herman Daly, "On Limiting Economic Growth," in D. L. Meadows, *Alternatives to Growth I*, 155–65.

19. The titles of their essays: Robert Allen, "Toward a Primary Lifestyle"; Bruce Hannon, "Economic Growth, Energy Use, and Altruism"; Joan Davis and Samuel Mauch, "Strategies for Societal Development"; and John Tanton, "International Migration and World Stability."

20. Orr, "An Inquiry into the Nature of Sustainable Societies," contains the

five Mitchell Prize papers from the 1977 Woodlands Conference.

21. Daly, "On Limiting Economic Growth," in D. L. Meadows, *Alternatives to Growth I*, 158.

22. D. L. Meadows, *Alternatives to Growth I*, xxii.

23. D. L. Meadows, *Alternatives to Growth I*, xxv–xxvi.

24. Mitchell interview, May 3, 2006.

25. Mitchell interviews, March 9, March 22, and May 3, 2006.

26. Mitchell interview, May 15, 1996, in Kutchin, *How Mitchell Energy and Development Corp. Got Its Start*, 427.

27. Mitchell interview, March 22, 2006.

28. Dennis Pirages, ed., *The Sustainable Society* (New York: Praeger, 1977).

29. See Simon Dresner, *The Principles of Sustainability* (London: Earthscan, 2002), 30.

30. See Appendix 1 for a list of the prizewinning papers for 1977.

31. Mitchell interview, May 3, 2006.

32. Allen Commander, cited in "Retrospective [on the Woodlands Conferences]," *The Woodlands Forum* (HARC Center for Global Studies) 10, no. 2 (Winter 1993–94): 9–10.

33. Harlan Cleveland and Thomas Wilson Jr., *Humangrowth: An Essay on Growth, Values, and the Quality of Life* (Aspen, Colo.: Aspen Institute for Humanistic Studies, 1978).

34. John McHale was an active participant during the planning stage of the 1979 conference. He died unexpectedly on November 2, 1978.

35. Meadows interview, March 14, 2007, p. 13.

36. Harlan Cleveland, ed., *The Management of Sustainable Growth* (New York: Pergamon Press, 1981), and James C.

Coomer, ed., *Quest for a Sustainable Society* (New York: Pergamon Press, 1981).

37. Harlan Cleveland, cited in "Retrospective [on the Woodlands Conferences]," *The Woodlands Forum* (HARC Center for Global Studies) 10, no. 2 (Winter 1993–94): 9.

38. Alexander King and Harlan Cleveland, eds., *Bioresources for Development: The Renewable Way of Life* (New York: Pergamon Press, 1980).

39. Orr, "An Inquiry into the Nature of Sustainable Societies," 6.

40. Harlan Cleveland, "We Changed Our Minds in the 1970s," in Cleveland, *Management of Sustainable Growth* 7.

41. Maurice F. Strong, "Action for New Growth," in Cleveland, *Management of Sustainable Growth*, 376.

42. Robert Chianese, "Gear-Bustin' through a Paradigm Shift," *The Woodlands Forum* (HARC Center for Global Studies) 10, no. 2 (Winter 1993–94): 6.

43. David Gottlieb, interview, August 23, 1995, in Kutchin, *How Mitchell Energy and Development Corp. Got Its Start*, 215.

44. From Paul Ehrlich's Web site, Stanford University, Center for Conservation Biology, Ecofables/ Ecoscience, "The Two Simon Bets," http://www.stanford.edu/group/CCB/ Pubs/Ecofablesdocs/thebet.htm (accessed February 15, 2010).

45. For a detailed account of the Ehrlich-Simon bet, see John Tierney, "Betting on the Planet," *New York Times Magazine*, December 2, 1990.

46. Susan Grinton Orr, ed., *An Inquiry into the Nature of Sustainable Societies: The Role of the Private Sector* (Houston: The Woodlands Center for Growth Studies, 1984).

47. Mitchell interview, March 9, 2006.

48. Mitchell interview, March 22, 2006.

49. Orr, "An Inquiry into the Nature of Sustainable Societies: A History of the Evolution and Content of the Woodlands Conference," 7.

50. Orr, *An Inquiry into the Nature of Sustainable Societies: The Role of the Private Sector*, 2.

51. Mitchell interview, March 22, 2006.

52. David Gottlieb, Joseph W. Kutchin, and Anthony R. Lentini, "A New Concept for the Woodlands Conferences," August 30, 1984, p. 1, mimeographed memorandum, MND-Devon Archives, Box 21860, Houston.

53. There are not many references to the Woodlands Conferences in the academic literature. An exception is Charles V. Kidd's "The Evolution of Sustainability."

54. Minutes of the Board of Directors of the Woodlands Conference held on April 28, 1983, p. 1, MND-Devon Archives, Box 21860, Houston.

55. Dennis Meadows to George Mitchell, letter, December 31, 1982, p. 2, MND-Devon Archives, Box 21860, Houston.

56. David Gottlieb in Kutchin, *How Mitchell Energy and Development Corp. Got Its Start*, 213.

57. Kutchin, *How Mitchell Energy and Development Corp.*, 215.

58. George P. Mitchell, undated memorandum (1974), MND-Devon Archives, Box 21860, Houston.

59. George P. Mitchell, interview by Jurgen Schmandt, April 5, 2006.

60. W. Arthur "Skip" Porter, interview, August 15, 1995, in Kutchin, *How Mitchell Energy and Development Corp.*, 503.

61. George P. Mitchell, letter to the president of HARC, July 31, 1985, HARC Files, The Woodlands, Tex.

Chapter 6. Washington Takes Note

1. Council on Environmental Quality and Department of State, *The Global 2000 Report to the President: Entering the Twenty-first Century* (Washington, D.C.: U.S. Government Printing Office, 1981), 1:5.

2. For a frank assessment of the difficulties encountered in preparing a multi-agency government report see Gerald Barney's preface to the Pergamon Press edition of *The Global 2000 Report to the President* (New York: Pergamon Press, 1980), vii–xvii.

3. *Global 2000 Report to the President* (Pergamon Press), 274.

4. *Global 2000 Report to the President* (U.S. Government Printing Office), 1:1.

5. *Global 2000 Report to the President*, 1:3.

6. Julian L. Simon and Herman Kahn, eds., *The Resourceful Earth: A Response to Global 2000* (New York: Blackwell, 1994), 3.

7. Frank Press, interview by Jurgen Schmandt, April 18, 2007, pp. 1–2.

8. Brand interview, March 27, 2007.

9. Mitchell interview, April 18, 2006.

10. Mitchell interview, April 5, 2006.

11. Gus Speth, personal communication, 1991.

12. World Resources Institute, *The Global Possible: The Statement and Action Agenda of an International Conference on Resources, Development, and the New Century* (Washington, D.C.: World Resources Institute, 1984).

13. World Resources Institute, *The Global Possible*, 3–4.

14. Robert Repetto, ed., *The Global*

Possible: Resources, Development, and the New Century, a World Resources Institute book (New Haven, Conn.: Yale University Press, 1985), 10.

Chapter 7. The Mitchell Center, 1984–2001

1. Jurgen Schmandt and Judith Clarkson, eds., *The Regions and Global Warming: Impacts and Response Strategies* (New York: Oxford University Press, 1992).

2. Daniel B. Botkin, "Global Warming and Forests of the Great Lake States: An Example of the Use of Quantitative Projections in Policy Analysis," in Schmandt and Clarkson, *Regions and Global Warming*, 154–66.

3. Botkin, "Global Warming and Forests of the Great Lake States," 154.

4. J. Schmandt, I. Aguilera-Barajas, M. Mathis, N. Armstrong, L. Chapa-Almena, S. Contreras-Balderas, R. Edwards, J. Hazleton, J. Navar-Chaidez, E. Vogel, and G. Ward, *Water and Sustainable Development in the Binational Lower Rio Grande/Río Bravo Basin*, Final Report to EPA/NSF Water and Watersheds Grant Program (grant no. R 824799-01-0), Houston Advanced Research Center, The Woodlands, TX, 2000, http://www.harc.edu/Projects/Archive/RioGrandeBravo/Report (accessed January 21, 2008); and I. Aguilar-Barajas, M. Mathis, and J. Schmandt, *Water Security and Economic Development in the Binational Rio Grande/Río Bravo Basin, USA/Mexico*, SIWI Report 13 (Stockholm: Stockholm International Water Institute, 2001), 79–87.

5. Public Policy Institute of California, "Managing California's Water Market: Issues and Prospects," Research Brief no. 74, July 2003, http://www.ppic

.org/content/pubs/rb/RB_703EHRB.pdf (accessed September 18, 2009).

6. Elinor Ostrom, *Governing the Commons: The Evolution of Institutions for Collective Action* (Cambridge: Cambridge University Press, 1990); and Elinor Ostrom, Thomas Dietz, Nives Dolšak, Paul C. Stern, Susan Stonich, and Elke U. Weber, eds., *The Drama of the Commons* (Washington, D.C.: National Academy Press, 2002).

7. Ostrom, *Governing the Commons*, 90.

8. Mitchell Lee Mathis, "Policy Design in an Imperfect World: Essays on the Management and Use of Open Access Renewable Resources" (Ph D thesis, University of Texas at Austin, 1999).

9. A full set of the ARIDAS working papers is available in the Bentsen Library of the Institute of Latin American Studies, University of Texas at Austin. Also see A. R. Magalhães, *Projecto ARIDAS: Uma Estrategia de Desenvolvimento Sustentável para o Nordeste* (Brasilia: Ministry of Planning, 1994), and A. Magalhães and J. Schmandt, *The Road to Sustainable Development* (Austin: Lyndon B. Johnson School of Public Affairs, 1998).

10. Sunil Tankha, ed., "Relocation and Resettlement in Ceará: Final Report on Findings and Recommendations to the Secretariat of Water Resources," State of Ceará, Brazil, 1999, http://files.harc.edu/Projects/Archive/Reports/RelocationResettlementCeara.pdf (accessed February 15, 2010).

11. J. D. Wilson, J. E. Kohlhase, and S. Strawn, "Quality of Life and Comparative Risk in Houston," *Urban Ecosystems* 3 (1999): 113–29.

12. Foresight Science Panel, *Houston Environment 1995* (The Woodlands, Tex.: Houston Advanced Research Center, 1996).

13. Foresight Committee, *Seeking Environmental Improvement* (The Woodlands, Tex.: Houston Advanced Research Center, 1996).

14. Houston Environmental Foresight, *Recommendations for Environmental Improvement: Report of Houston Environmental Foresight Air Quality Work Group*, January 2000, http://files.harc.edu/Projects/Archive/Foresight/OutdoorAndIndoorAir.pdf; *Report of Houston Environmental Foresight Habitat, Parks and Water Issues Work Group*, January 2000, http://files.harc.edu/Projects/Archive/Foresight/HabitatParksAndWater.pdf; *Report of Houston Environmental Toxins and Contaminants Work Group*, March 2000, http://files.harc.edu/Projects/Archive/Foresight/ToxinsDraft.pdf (all reports accessed February 17, 2008).

15. Jurgen Schmandt, "Civic Science," *Science Communication* 20 (1998): 62–69.

Chapter 8. National Academy of Sciences

1. Letter, George P. Mitchell to Gerald O. Barney, January 26, 1983, MND-Devon Archives, Box 22831, Houston.

2. Wirth later became director of the United Nations Foundation.

3. George P. Mitchell, interview, *The Woodlands Forum* 10, no. 2 (Winter 1993–94): 4.

4. United States Congress, Senate and House of Representatives, "An Act to Incorporate the National Academy of Sciences," March 3, 1863, National Academy of Sciences, http://www.nasonline.org/site/PageServer?pagename=ABOUT_incorporation (accessed February 15, 2010).

5. Rexmond Canning Cochrane, *National Academy of Sciences: The First Hundred Years, 1863–1963* (Washington, D.C.: National Academy Press, 1978).

6. Cabell Brand, interview by Jurgen Schmandt, March 7, 2007, p. 15.

7. Brand interview, March 7, 2007; Press interview, April 18, 2007.

8. William Colglazier, interview by Jurgen Schmandt, March 6, 2007.

9. Mitchell interview, April 18, 2006.

10. This first Mitchell grant to the National Academy was provided by Mitchell Energy and Development Corporation and the Cynthia and George Mitchell Foundation.

11. Pamela Matson, interview by Jurgen Schmandt, April 20, 2007.

12. The President's Council on Sustainable Development advised President Clinton from 1993 to 1999. For details see http://clinton2.nara.gov/PCSD/ (accessed January 31, 2008). The World Business Council for Sustainable Development was created in 1992 by Bernd Schmidheiny of Switzerland. For details see http://www.wbcsd.org/templates/TemplateWBCSD2/layout.asp?type=p&MenuId=NDEx&doOpen=1&ClickMenu=LeftMenu (accessed January 31, 2008).

13. Board on Sustainable Development, *Our Common Journey: A Transition toward Sustainability* (Washington, D.C.: National Research Council, 1999), xiv.

14. Robert W. Kates, personal communication, 1995.

15. Matson interview, April 20, 2007.

16. Ralph Cicerone, interview by Jurgen Schmandt, March 15, 2007.

17. Cicerone interview, March 15, 2007.

18. William C. Clark and Nancy M. Dickson, "Sustainability Science: The

Emerging Research Program," *Proceedings of the National Academy of Sciences of the United States* 100, no. 14 (July 8, 2003): 8060.

19. Matson interview, April 20, 2007.

20. Mitchell interview, May 3, 2006.

21. Jurgen Schmandt and C. H. Ward, eds., *Sustainable Development: The Challenge of Transition* (Cambridge: Cambridge University Press, 2000).

22. Schmandt and Ward, *Sustainable Development*, xiii–xiv.

23. Robert W. Kates, "Population and Consumption: From More to Enough," in Schmandt and Ward, *Sustainable Development*, 79.

24. Kates, "Population and Consumption," 96.

25. HARC press release, March 4, 1997.

26. HARC, Center for Global Studies, *Corporate Incentives and Environmental Decision Making* (The Woodlands, Tex.: HARC, 1999).

27. Paul Hawken, *The Ecology of Commerce: A Declaration of Sustainability* (New York: Harper Business, 1993).

28. Ray C. Anderson, *Mid-Course Correction: Toward a Sustainable Enterprise: The Interface Model* (White River Junction, Vt.: Chelsea Green, 1998); "Case Study 27, Interface," in Charles O. Holliday Jr., Stephan Schmidheiny, Philip Watts, and World Business Council for Sustainable Development, *Walking the Talk: The Business Case for Sustainable Development* (San Francisco: Berrett-Koehler, 2002), 142.

29. Anderson, *Mid-Course Correction*, 73.

30. Anderson, *Mid-Course Correction*, 73.

Chapter 9. The New Houston Advanced Research Center (HARC)

1. The schism between two organizational cultures was first examined by C. P. Snow, *The Two Cultures* (Cambridge: Cambridge University Press, 1968).

2. The strategic plan is summarized in the HARC brochure, The Woodlands, 2006, http://files.harc.edu/WWW/HARCBrochure.pdf (accessed February 15, 2010).

3. For details, see chapter 8.

4. David H. Guston, "Stabilizing the Boundary between U.S. Politics and Science: The Role of the Office of Technology Transfer as a Boundary Organization," *Social Studies of Science* 29, no. 1 (February 1999): 87–111.

5. David W. Cash, William C. Clark, Frank Alcock, Nancy M. Dickson, Noelle Eckley, David H. Guston, Jill Jäger, and Ronald B. Mitchell, "Knowledge Systems for Sustainable Development" in *Proceedings of the National Academy of Sciences* 100, no. 14 (July 8, 2003): 8086–91.

6. Robert C. Harriss, Testimony before the Subcommittee on Energy and Environment, House Committee on Science and Technology, Hearing on "Energizing Houston: Sustainability, Technological Innovation, and Growth in the Energy Capital of the World," 110th Cong., 2nd sess., February 29, 2008.

7. The Greater Houston Partnership comprises three divisions: Chamber of Commerce, Economic Development, and World Trade. For details about the Texas Environmental Research Consortium, see http://www.tercairquality.org/About/ (accessed March 4, 2008).

8. Texas Environmental Research Consortium, *Annual Report 2007*, p. 3, http://files.harc.edu/Sites/TERC/About/AnnualReport200701.pdf (accessed February 16, 2010).

Chapter 10. The Mitchell Paradox

1. Mitchell interview, April 5, 2006.
2. Mitchell interview, April 18, 2006.
3. Mitchell interview, April 18, 2006.

Chapter 11. Mitchell's Impact and Legacy

1. Mitchell interview, April 5, 2006.
2. Mitchell interview, April 18, 2006.
3. Mitchell interview, April 5, 2006.
4. Frank Press interview, April 18, 2007.
5. Mitchell interview, April 18, 2006.
6. From the Web page of the Roundtable on Science and Technology for Sustainability, "Sustainability at the National Academies," National Academy of Sciences, http://sustainability.nationalacademies.org/roundtable.shtml (accessed March 19, 2008).
7. Cicerone interview, March 15, 2007.
8. Mitchell interview, April 5, 2006.
9. Mitchell interview, April 5, 2006.
10. Mitchell interview, April 5, 2006.
11. Matson interview, April 20, 2007.

INDEX